The
Amazing
Queen

Winning With
Your Queens

Clement Wong
王啓明

HNB Publishing   •   New York

Bridge books available from HNB Publishing

Demon Defense and Demon Doubling: Defend With Skill and Double for Keeps
(Advanced Intermediate)

Three Notrump in Depth
(Advanced Intermediate)

Wielding the Axe: The Vanishing Art of the Penalty Double
(Advanced Intermediate)

Matchpoints Versus IMPs: Different Games, Different Strategies
(Advanced Intermediate)

Private Sessions
(Beginner)

ISBN: 978-0-9828874-9-3

The publisher offers discounts on books ordered in bulk quantities.

HNB Publishing
250 W. 78th St., #3FF
New York, NY 10024
www.hnbpub.com

Current printing (last digit):

10 9 8 7 6 5 4 3 2

PRINTED IN THE UNITED STATES

PREFACE

W hile finalizing this book, I was watching the latest international bridge events. The crucial hands that decided the winners looked familiar. Many were similar to those that I selected from my collection of around 2,000 memorable hands featuring world champions and experts, and that are presented here in print for the first time.

The hands in this book feature players from all continents—many of them well-known names—performing brilliantly and sometimes not so brilliantly. Obviously, I played a few of the hands myself. The lessons that these hands demonstrate by example (and counterexample) can benefit a wide range of bridge players, from club players to world-class experts.

As you may have deduced from the title, the book's common thread is queens. My fascination with queens goes back to my 1993 Bols Tip of Queening Your Defence, which introduced the idea of queen hiding and seeking with declarers. It incorporated dropping your queen—a real or sham sacrifice—to divert declarer from his winning line. In 2010, the International Bridge Press Association awards for best declarer play and best defence went to a queen sacrifice similar to my tip. I decided to fulfill my mission to publish a bridge book on the subject.

Chapters 1 and 2 touch on broad areas—bidding and declarer play—and the next three chapters address more specific topics—opening leads and responses, ruffing, and entries—but in all five chapters, the special role of queens is explored. The final three chapters cover queen defence, queen play, and trump soldiers, and build on the technique of my Bols Tip. Every chapter begins with relevant tips and explains possibly unfamiliar queen vocabulary.

Tips are not formulas. Nevertheless, I have re-tested the tips in recent international tournaments and they work well. To understand my Bols Tip and the vocabulary, take the example of Queen Sacrifice. In an endplay, defender holds Qxx, dummy has K109, and declarer has Axx. He sacrifices the queen to protect partner's jack. Likewise, holding Q10x opposite dummy's 98x, a defender sacrifices the queen in an endplay for two tricks when declarer to your left holds AJx. A further example is Queen (King) Hiding, the skill of hiding a crucial queen (king). I have witnessed experts revealing too many high cards, thereby exposing partner's off-side singleton king. This book assumes some advanced skills surrounding queens and, to a lesser extent, kings and jacks. Coups include Emperor, Deschapelles, Bath, Morton, and others.

I wish to thank the publisher for printing this work and the players who have played with or against me. I have had the good fortune of playing against world champions in qualifying rounds—and the even better fortune of never having lost to one. Their complimentary comments remain in my heart. I hope you enjoy this book, which is dedicated to players who would like to "Queen" their bidding, play, lead, defence, and overall enjoyment of bridge.

Clement Wong
Hong Kong

CONTENTS

1

THE EXPLORER

TIPS FOR
Bidding

- Read this chapter—for that matter, this book—with partners.
- Win by queening your bidding and play.
- Discuss bidding styles with partners.
- Upgrade your hand with honours in sequence.
- Upgrade you hand with 10's and 9's.
- Be creative with your take-out doubles.
- Explore by bidding rather than passing.
- Consider a lower bid in noncompetitive situations.
- Consider a higher bid in competitive situations.
- Bid a 5-card major before a 6-card minor.
- Open subminimum no-trumps.
- Cue bid before asking key cards.
- Count slams tricks with crucial queens.
- Overcall strong 1-clubs.
- Overcall relay bids.
- Refrain from a penalty double with a balanced hand.
- Refrain from announcing good trumps with a penalty double.
- Prepare a defence against no-trump openings.
- Prepare conventions in competitive situations.
- Prepare a defence against conventions and new gadgets.

Swings hinge on difficult-to-reach, but odds-on games and slams. It is vital for you and your partner to explore them through bidding. The hands in this chapter feature off-shape doubles and unbalanced openings, slams with one ace and meager strength, raising a doubled 6♡ to 7♡—and making it, and opening seven with two holes. There are also lessons on part-score doubles and conventions. As with all hands in this book, the winning decisions involve evaluation of crucial queens.

Winning through skillful bids and card play surrounding the queens draws upon new strategies and new vocabulary. We'll introduce each chapter with the relevant vocabulary:

Queening

Win by skillful bidding and play surrounding the queens.

Queening

Queen bid

Evaluate your queens to reach the par contract.

Queen bid

Queen run

Assess the distribution of the queens before switching contracts.

Queen run

An off-shape double

		♠ Q864	
2009 BBO Internet		♡ J8764	
IMP pairs		◇ 852	
W/ NS vulnerable		♣ 3	

	♠ 975		♠ K2
	♡ 52		♡ AQ103
	◇ A97		◇ KQJ106
	♣ QJ1094		♣ 74

		♠ AJ103	
		♡ K9	
		◇ 43	
		♣ AK852	

West	*North*	*East*	*South*
China	Netherlands	USA	Clement
Pass	Pass	1◇	Double
Pass	1♡	2◇	Pass
Pass	2♠	Pass	4♠
5◇	Pass	Pass	Double

Many Internet players at Bridge Base Online (BBO) do not reveal their true names or countries. As you will notice for many of these hands, players sometimes identify themselves only as "Expert" or "World class." Playing with first-time partners at BBO, I used to choose an expert table. They would usually play a natural 5-card-major system with 2♣ as the strong bid. Weak 2-bids, transfers after no-trumps, key-card Blackwood, and negative doubles to 3♠, or even higher, were the norm.

When I met opponents playing a strong-club system I overcalled light, sometimes with two-suited conventions, to occupy their valuable bidding space. This was the weak link of these systems, and the reason behind a virtual end to the forcing-pass system. In this hand, an overcall of 1♠ or 2♣ was deficient. I elected an off-shape double. The risk was lower when the higher suit was spades. North bid twice with a queen and a jack. Matching his vigour was West, who sacrificed in 5◊. 4♠ had three losers and not enough winners. Declarer could ruff a second club and played a spade to his jack. He cashed the ace of spades and ruffed two clubs in dummy. The tally was six trumps, two clubs, and the ♡A—one short of making the contract.

In 5◊ doubled, I resisted the tempting lead of the ace of clubs and led a trump to cut down ruffs in dummy. Declarer put up the ace in dummy, an error. He led the queen of clubs to my king. I led another diamond to the king. Declarer led a club and I put up the 8, signaling for a spade return, expecting North to ruff. North petered in trumps.

North ruffed and promptly returned a small spade to the king and my ace. I led a small spade to North's queen. North returned a heart and declarer guessed, putting up the queen, losing to my king. He ruffed a heart in dummy and lost another heart for down four, minus 800. My attempt to create entries to partner worked. He reinforced the defence with his lone queen and lone jack. Declarer could have gone down less by a skillful play surrounding his queens, or by leading clubs from his hand.

This hand illustrates that take-out doubles are sometimes dictated by high cards and not by promising unbid suits. In the 2011 China Elite Tournament, many international experts converted their partner's unbeatable 3NT to a failed 4♠. Partner doubled with 21 points and a singleton spade.

A long-suit double

2008 BBO Internet	♠ K
IMP pairs	♡ 82
W/ Both vulnerable	◇ K10654
	♣ 109765

	♠ Q1084		♠ 32
	♡ K643		♡ QJ1095
	◇ A7		◇ QJ98
	♣ A82		♣ 43

	♠ AJ9765
	♡ A7
	◇ 32
	♣ KQJ

West	North	East	South
World class	Expert	World class	Clement
1♣	Pass	1♡	Double
2♡	3◇	Double	3♠
4♡	Pass	Pass	Double

I thought my hand too strong for an overcall. A take-out double would be less risky with a spade suit. Partner competed voluntarily to 3◇, inviting a double by East. 3♠ had five losers. Fortunately, the bid pushed West to try a game in hearts. I doubted whether a world-class player would bid like West or East. Their bids defied the Queen Bid principle. They should discount their queens in the major suits.

4♡ went down two, minus 10 IMPs, losing two spades and one trick each in the other suits. My take-out double induced misconceptions for the opponents. They construed my hand to be rich in spades and diamonds. West thought the double of 3◇ by East showed strength. As my partner showed strength in diamonds, I was confident doubling 4♡.

A formula for 3NT

		♠ 75	
2009 BBO Internet		♡ AQ	
IMP pairs		◇ Q5	
N/ Both vulnerable		♣ QJ109863	

	♠ A		♠ Q109862
	♡ K1087		♡ 32
	◇ J98432		◇ AK6
	♣ 52		♣ AK

		♠ KJ43	
		♡ J9654	
		◇ 107	
		♣ 74	

West	North	East	South
		Clement	
	1♣	Double	1♡
2◇	Pass	2♠	Pass
3◇	Pass	3NT	

   This hand shows another effective take-out double with a hand strong in one suit. Instead of overcalling 1♠, I chose to double. (It's good practice to inform a new partner of your style in take-out doubles.) Many overcalled 1♠ and jumped in the next round, even with a doubtful queen-headed broken suit, landing in a hopeless game in spades.

   After two voluntary bids in diamonds by partner and lack of support in hearts from North, I was confident that partner had reasonable diamonds and positional stoppers in hearts. This was a magical match with my hand, a formula for 3NT. Of 16 tables, only ours bid the no-trump game. It was fortunate that diamonds broke 2-2. If there was an adverse break, the king of hearts might be on side for nine tricks.

Stranger in the night

		♠ 543	
2009 BBO Internet		♡ 9763	
IMP pairs		◊ 42	
S/ Neither vulnerable		♣ J432	

♠ A1098			♠ J76
♡ KQ108			♡ —
◊ A95			◊ QJ8763
♣ 97			♣ A1065

		♠ KQ2	
		♡ AJ542	
		◊ K10	
		♣ KQ8	

West	North	East	South
Clement	Expert	Expert	Expert
			1♡
Double	Pass	3◊	Pass
3NT			

Few would take-out double as West, who held opener's suit. The alternative was a 1♠ overcall with four cards. (As with take-out doubles, your partner should be aware of your style for overcalls.) We were strangers in the night. I felt I could stand a minor suit response from partner. If opponents played a weak jump-raise after a take-out double, they might silence East. However, they could be in trouble if East made a responsive double, as I would pass. After 3◊, 3NT was the value bid, as partner should have strength in clubs.

Unaware of my strong stoppers, North naturally led a heart. South played his ace and returned a heart to my king. I played the ◊A and a small diamond. There was no defence and we scored 430, the only table of 16 playing 3NT. Even if North had chosen the best lead of a club, declarer would still score nine tricks investigating diamonds. Three tables bid and made 5◊.

Many seated West passed in the first round, making it difficult for East-West to reach a game. They ignored upgrading their hands, having two tens, three nines, two eights, and the ♡KQ108 behind an opening 1♡. These cards were critical for success in a 21-point 3NT.

Running with Forrest Gump

2009 Yeh Brothers Cup final	♠ AJ6		
Netherlands v Sweden	♡ AQ53		
S/ Neither vulnerable	◊ A		
	♣ A10973		

♠ 95	♠ KQ1032
♡ KJ97	♡ 1042
◊ K975	◊ J103
♣ K84	♣ 62

♠ 874
♡ 86
◊ Q8642
♣ QJ5

West	North	East	South
Bakkeren	Nystrom	Bertens	Bertheau
			Pass
Pass	1♣	1♠	Pass
Pass	1NT	Pass	Pass
Double	Redouble	2◊	Double
Pass	Pass	2♠	Pass
Pass	Double		

Fredin	Drijver	Fallenius	Brink
			Pass
Pass	1♣	Pass	1◊
1♡	1NT		

Styles of overcalls vary. Bidding at the second table was relatively quiet: 1NT scored 120. At the first table, the light overcall backfired. East ran from 1NT redoubled to 2◊ (doubled), then to 2♠ (doubled).

South led the eight of hearts to the jack and queen. North cashed the ace of diamonds and ace of hearts, and led a heart. South ruffed and led the queen of clubs, covered by the king and ace. North returned a club to partner's jack, and ruffed the return of a diamond. North then played his last heart. Declarer ruffed with the 10. South discarded a club. Declarer played the king of spades to the ace. North led a third club. South overruffed declarer for five down, plus 1100.

This was the first session. Netherlands bounced back, winning by over 100 IMPs to collect US $76,000. East-West could have made a Queen Run. The lack of side queens incapacitated declarer. 2♡ or 2◊ or 1NT redoubled would have been less damaging. If East, having equal length in the unbid suits, had passed the redouble, South or West might have bid. Alternatively, East could have bid 2♣ and let West run. In the movie *Forrest Gump*, the title character ran effectively. East could have mitigated the damage by recognizing the stronger runner and making North lead. In the 2011 European Open Championship, a world champion pair ran from 1♡ to 1NT, to 2♣, and to 2◊ for down six, minus 1400. Their teammates played 5◊, minus 50. 2♣ would have been minus 500; 1♡ would have been minus 800.

Spotting spot cards

2007 Bermuda Cup final
Norway v USA2
S/ Neither vulnerable

	North		
	♠ K86		
	♡ 543		
	◊ KQ965		
	♣ 74		

West		East
♠ QJ743		♠ —
♡ 97		♡ AQJ2
◊ A32		◊ J1074
♣ QJ8		♣ K10962

	South		
	♠ A10952		
	♡ K1086		
	◊ 8		
	♣ A53		

West	North	East	South
Helgemo	*Garner*	*Helness*	*Weinstein*
			1♠
Pass	2♠	Double	Pass
2NT (minor)	Pass	3♣	
Zia	Tundal	Rosenberg	Groetheim
			1♠
Pass	2♠	Double	

This was a significant hand in the final. It was tempting for West to pass after a take-out double of 2♠. The small spot cards of ♠743 and the lack of a top honour in spades were worries, and holding a balanced hand, West would not be able to score trumps effectively. Helgemo decided to request Helness to declare in a minor suit, the Queen Run. In 3♣, South led his singleton diamond. Declarer played small from dummy. North took with his queen and returned a club. South ducked to the eight in dummy. Declarer passed the nine of hearts to the ten. South cashed the ace of clubs and led a third round. Declarer had losers in the red kings for minus 50.

In the other room, Zia sat West. He passed the double of 2♠, declared by Groetheim. West led a heart, partner's suit, to the jack and king. Declarer advanced his lone diamond. West rose up with his ace and led a second heart to the queen. East cashed the ace of hearts. West discarded a diamond. East attacked clubs. Declarer took with his ace. He led the ten of spades, covered by the jack and king. Declarer pitched two clubs on the king and queen of diamonds. West ruffed the queen and scored one more trump trick. Declarer made his contract, gaining 10 IMPs. If West does not play the ace on the first diamond, declarer should score five trump tricks, fulfilling his contract. While the positions of the red queens were crucial, the black queens in West were ineffective.

Norway defeated USA to become world champion for the first time. They had previously lost two tight finals, to Netherlands in 1993, and to USA2 in 2001. In 2009, Zia won his first world team championship.

Landy for a brave heart

2009 BBO Internet		♠ J102	
IMP pairs		♡ K4	
N/ EW vulnerable		◇ KQ543	
		♣ KQ7	

	♠ A97		♠ KQ65
	♡ 10852		♡ AJ963
	◇ —		◇ J98
	♣ J86543		♣ 2

		♠ 843	
		♡ Q7	
		◇ A10762	
		♣ A109	

West	*North*	*East*	*South*
Expert	Clement	Expert	Expert
	1NT	Pass	3NT

The queens were instrumental to my success in this hand. My queens, cohabiting with the kings, were a bonus. I upgraded my hand a point to bid 1NT. I would normally have better diamonds for this bid, or more tens and nines. The favourable vulnerability and the lack of major suits urged me to a bid more blocking than 1◊. East could venture a Landy convention for the majors. Being vulnerable, he opted to pass. Some openers bid 1NT with a six-card minor. Holding a singleton, East could miss a vulnerable game.

The natural lead of a heart provided me the ninth trick. I was lucky to find two relevant aces in partner and escaped the lead of a spade, which would be down one. As defenders had nine hearts, they should not complain about the lead. Half of the field and eight tables were in 4♡ East-West. Five tables sacrificed in 5◊ doubled, down two. We were the only North-South with a plus score.

Michaels with a Yarborough

2009 Venice Cup semi-final
France v China
S/ NS vulnerable

	♠ J10875	
	♡ 109742	
	◇ 97	
	♣ 5	

♠ 43		♠ A2
♡ J6		♡ K85
◇ KQJ42		◇ 10863
♣ Q932		♣ KJ74

	♠ KQ96	
	♡ AQ3	
	◇ A5	
	♣ A1086	

West	North	East	South
Willard	*Sun*	*Cronier*	*H L Wang*
			1♣ (Precision, 16+)
2◇	Pass	2NT	Pass
3♣	3◇ (majors)	5◇	Double

Liu	D'Ovidio	W F Wang	Gaviard
			1♣
1◇	Pass	2NT	

This was the fifth of six sessions. France was ahead by over 20 IMPs. In the first room, 3◇ was Michaels for majors. It was an effective convention and a brave bid. The bids of 2◇ and 3♣ by West, announcing her two queens, alerted North of prospects in the majors. Before South responded the likely 4♠, East applied pressure by bidding 5◇. South guessed right by doubling. North led her singleton in clubs and received a ruff. Her return of a spade allowed declarer to put up the ace. Declarer drew trumps and conceded down four, minus 800. If North had returned a heart after the ruff in clubs, the result would have been minus 1100.

In the other room, the bidding was natural. North needed more courage to compete. It was not clear if they adopted Michaels at this position. The competition by East-West silenced their opponents. 2NT went down three, but China gained 12 IMPs. The Precision bidding worked better in this hand. China recovered 53 IMPs in this session. After countless misses since a bronze in 1991, China defeated France and then USA to become world champions for the first time.

The three-five preempt

2009 Transnational Team final	♠ AKQ9	
Zimmermann v Poland	♡ 6	
W/ Neither vulnerable	◇ AK873	
	♣ A109	

	♠ 3		♠ 87542
	♡ KQJ952		♡ 10843
	◇ 52		◇ 9
	♣ J843		♣ KQ2

		♠ J106	
		♡ A7	
		◇ QJ1064	
		♣ 765	

West	North	East	South
Helgemo	Pczczola	Helness	Gawrys
3♡	Double	5♡	Double
Narkiewicz	Balicki	Buras	Zmudzinski
2◇	Double	4◇	Double
4♡	6◇		

In the Bermuda Bowl final, both Italy and USA bid the slam in diamonds. North-South in the second room also bid the slam in two rounds of bidding. After drawing trumps, the fourth spade pitched a club loser for an easy twelve tricks. In the first room, East-West bid a simple 3♡–5♡. It was fashionable to pre-empt at the three-level with a good six-card suit, and to raise to the five-level with a moderately weak hand. A double of 5♡ sounded like penalties. A double of 4◊ in the second room sounded like take-out.

5♡ went down two, minus 300. The slam gained 12 IMPs. The multinational squad, with Multon, won the final. The Polish North in the first room, needing a relevant king and queen from partner, could try a 5NT over 5♡. If partner bid 6♣, he could bid 6◊, pinpointing a second suit in spades.

In a Hong Kong international event, declarer held ♠AKQ9 ♡AKJ1074 ◊AK ♣A. He heard 3♣ to his left and 6♣ to his right. Missing the queen of hearts, he bid 7♡, down one. If he had bid 7♣—the Queen Bid—partner would have bid 7◊ and converted his 7♡ to an ironclad 7♠. Partner had four spades and two hearts. Opponents won the match, staying in 6♡. The three-five or three-six preempt denied opponents bidding space. It simulated a weak raise to the three-level of a suit, denying opponents a cue bid to explore 3NT.

An unbalanced opening

2008 BBO Internet	♠ 7653		
IMP pairs	♡ K8642		
N/ NS vulnerable	◇ KQ6		
	♣ 3		

♠ —		♠ AJ1084	
♡ 975		♡ 3	
◇ AJ10432		◇ 5	
♣ KQ85		♣ AJ10742	

	♠ KQ92		
	♡ AQJ10		
	◇ 987		
	♣ 96		

West	North	East	South
Expert	Expert	Clement	Expert
	Pass	1♠	Double
Pass	3♡	4♣	Pass
5♣	5♡	Pass	Pass
6♣	Double		

The take-out double is not a popular choice: it carries risks. I once succeeded with a double similar to South's, leading to a difficult-to-reach 3NT. My four-card suit in that hand was in spades. Here South had good spot cards. North was ignorant of South's shape. He got overexcited pushing opponents. West refrained from bidding after the take-out double, but he competed vigorously after my voluntary 4♣.

Many champions bid a five-card major before a six-card minor. This hand showed the advantage of this strategy; otherwise, North could bid 4♣ over 1♣—Double—1◇, asking South to pick a major. West was prevented from judging subsequent responses, as I could open 1♣ with two cards. West detected my heart shortage, making the expert Queen Bid of 6♣. His queen of clubs was the catalyst. It compensated my unbalanced 1♠ opening, masking the longer clubs.

South showed his expert status by leading a trump, although he missed a heart trick. I played the ace of diamonds and ruffed a diamond with a high trump. I drew another trump with the king and ruffed another diamond. The good diamonds pitched a loser in hearts. I had eight trump tricks, four diamonds, and the ace of spades, for an overtrick and 1190. Of 16 tables, we were the only pair to bid a slam.

Norwegian wood

1997 Bermuda Bowl	♠ K2	
Norway v Italy	♡ KJ83	
E/ Both vulnerable	◇ AJ105	
	♣ AK7	

♠ Q	♠ J843
♡ A1092	♡ 7654
◇ 864	◇ 972
♣ Q6542	♣ J3

♠ A109765
♡ Q
◇ KQ3
♣ 1098

West	North	East	South
Duboin	Helness	Bocchi	Helgemo
		Pass	1♠
Pass	2◇	Pass	2♠
Pass	3♣	Pass	3◇
Pass	3♠	Pass	4♣ (waiting, last train)
Pass	4NT (ask)	Pass	5◇ (1 key card)
Pass	5♡ (ask)	Pass	5♠ (no ♠Q)
Pass	6◇		

For this hand, the key is to think of a lower bid in a non-competitive situation: for example, 4♣. After a natural sequence and asking bids, Helness judged that as Helgemo had one ace and denied having the queen of spades, he ought to have one king and two queens. Helgemo supported diamonds and bid 4♣, showing slam interest. He should hold ♦KQx. Helness steered to the only makable slam in a Moysian fit with a Queen Bid.

East led a heart to the ace. West returned a club to the ace. Declarer ruffed a heart in dummy. He crossed to his king of clubs, played the king of hearts, discarding a club in dummy. He led his third club for a ruff in dummy with the queen. After playing the king of diamonds and king of spades, he drew trumps and claimed 1370. Norway won the match, but had to wait till 2007 to become world champions.

Slam with a single ace

2008 BBO Internet
IMP pairs
W/ Neither vulnerable

	♠ AJ7	
	♡ KQJ109	
	◊ —	
	♣ K6532	

♠ 62		♠ 9
♡ A82		♡ 643
◊ AQ543		◊ J1096
♣ A108		♣ QJ974

	♠ KQ108543	
	♡ 75	
	◊ K872	
	♣ —	

West	*North*	*East*	*South*
Expert	Advanced	Expert	Clement
1◊	1♡	Pass	1♠
2◊	4♠	Pass	5♣
Pass	6♣	Pass	6♠
Double			

I prefer cue bids before using Blackwood. My bidding options in the first round ranged from 1♠ to 4♠. My humble 1♠ allowed bidding space. After 4♠, I felt partner should have two first-round controls and tried a delicate 5♣. Being an advanced player, his raise to 6♣ was understandable. West, holding three aces, could not resist doubling an ironclad 6♠. He did expertly well to lead a trump. Taking in hand, I led the nine of hearts. West ducked. I continued with the ten. It did not matter when West took his ace. If East had doubleton hearts and ruffed the third round, the defence had no more trumps and dummy could ruff twice.

I played fast, risking a singleton heart in East. This was unlikely based on the bidding and lead. But I should have drawn two rounds of trumps and forced out the ace of hearts. On any return, I came to hand and ruffed a diamond with the last trump in dummy. Three good hearts discarded three losing diamonds, scoring 980.

The location of the king of diamonds scared many at South from exploring slam. The exploration required was actually the queens in the majors. After 5♣, North should know the powerful spades and club controls in South. If he bid 5◊ and his partner could not bid 5♡, he could settle for six. His bid of 6♣, catering for a club fit and forcing to 6♠, was arguably world class. Our table was the only one to reach a slam.

Jump before you leap

2007 BBO Internet
IMP pairs
S/ Neither vulnerable

```
                    ♠ AKQ762
                    ♡ A976
                    ◊ —
                    ♣ 742
       ♠ 103                      ♠ 954
       ♡ 105                      ♡ QJ43
       ◊ AK108765                 ◊ 32
       ♣ J3                       ♣ 10986
                    ♠ J8
                    ♡ K82
                    ◊ QJ94
                    ♣ AKQ5
```

West	North	East	South
	Clement		
			1NT
3◊	6♠		

The bidding took ten seconds. After the 1NT–3◊ jump, the strength in the four hands was crystal clear. Clubs were a slight worry. Partner should hold the relevant queens and kings. An immediate leap to 6♠ would receive a diamond lead and advantages in tempo. A third of the field bid a slam.

I ruffed the lead of a diamond and played the king and ace of hearts. I floated a third heart to East. He returned the fourth heart. I ruffed with the jack. A 3-2 break in trumps allowed the slam home. The play took less than a minute, the quickest table. With a trump lead, I drew trumps, ducked a heart, and squeezed East in hearts and clubs.

This hand shows the power of a six-card suit headed by the AKQ. We should jump-bid after a two-level response from partner; for example, 1♠-2◊-3♠. In many international tournaments, including the 2011 Spingold Teams, many champions missed slams when they bid only 2♠ in the second round.

Raising a doubled small slam

2008 BBO Internet	♠ QJ976
IMP pairs	♡ 54
N/ Neither vulnerable	◊ Q95
	♣ 932

	♠ 105		♠ 8432
	♡ 92		♡ 7
	◊ J876		◊ 1042
	♣ AK854		♣ QJ1076

	♠ AK
	♡ AKQJ10863
	◊ AK3
	♣ —

West	North	East	South
	Pass	Pass	6♡
Double	7♡	Pass	Pass
Double			

Queens were critical in this hand. Many at South opened their hand 6♡ or 7♡, unscientifically. The double of 6♡ revealed important hints. I deduced that West should not have two aces for his double. The opener could be void in one of his aces. He would not double with a lone ace. A good suit with AK was more likely. Even if declarer was singleton in his suit, his partner might have a trick. As I possessed the queens in spades and diamonds, chances were that West held the club suit.

If my partner did have a singleton club and no more losers, he had A or AK bare in spades and diamonds—unlikely. My queens were a perfect match for his holes in spades and diamonds. The risk was a doubleton ace in a suit. Rather than a redouble, I ventured 7♡, the Queen Bid. As expected, West reiterated his double. It was unforgettable to bid and make a doubled grand slam, having been penalty-doubled in a small slam of the same suit. A redouble would have been extravagant. We scored the top IMP. Half of the field went to the grand, mostly by opening 7♡, and none by the 6♡-7♡ route. 6♡ doubled would have scored negative IMPs.

A grand opening

2008 BBO Internet   ♠ 10872
IMP pairs   ♡ J875
S/ Both vulnerable   ◊ KJ873
     ♣ —

	♠ J5		♠ 43
	♡ AQ64		♡ K10932
	◊ Q1094		◊ 652
	♣ 875		♣ 432

     ♠ AKQ96
     ♡ —
     ◊ A
     ♣ AKQJ1096

West	*North*	*East*	*South*
Expert	Expert	Expert	Clement
			7♣

In the well-over 40 years since I had been playing bridge, I had never been dealt such a magnificent hand. I greeted its birth with a delicate 7♣ opening. I had two holes in spades, but the queen raised aspirations. Regardless of the number of spades in my partner, my grand slam stood a good chance of success. The worst chance was with two spades only in partner, but then a moderate trump spot in partner would suffice. As described earlier, when the bidding came to a strong hand, the opponents had reached the five- or six-level preemptively. As opponents might have an abundance of red cards and shortages in the black suits, a 2♣ strong opening risked interference. When the bidding came back to South, bidding six in the reds as a cheap sacrifice was a distinct possibility.

It happened that opponents had balanced hands. A strong opening by South led to a grand slam. The difficulty was that South had to jump to 4♣ in the second round. After a bid of 4♦ from North, and 4♠ or 6♠ from South, North would raise spades. There were still some happy endings: about 60% of the field bid a grand slam. Naturally, this was the first time I ever opened at the seven-level. There was no assurance of thirteen tricks when I bid it. To make it was ecstasy and a dream come true.

The law of grand slam

2009 China	♠ AQJ82	
National championship	♡ AJ	
S/ Neither vulnerable	◊ J3	
	♣ A1076	

♠ 1073		♠ 96
♡ 1095		♡ K87
◊ Q10986		◊ AK7542
♣ 53		♣ 82

	♠ K54	
	♡ Q6432	
	◊ —	
	♣ KQJ94	

West	North	East	South
	Sun		H L Wang
			1♡
Pass	1♠	Pass	2♣
Pass	2◊ (4th suit)	Pass	2♠ (3 card)
Pass	3♣ (support)	Pass	4◊ (singleton or void)
Pass	4NT (ask)	Pass	5NT (odd number
Pass	7♠		of key cards +
			useful void)

After a bronze in 1991, many silvers, and near misses, the China ladies won two world championships in 2009 and 2010. Only Sun and Wang played in both events. They demonstrated a law of total tricks in slams. Eight trumps scored more tricks than nine.

2◊ was game forcing. 5NT stated the diamond void and one key card in spades. Sun deduced that South was 3-5-0-5. If South had ♡KQ, her club losers went away; if she had ♣KQ, her heart losers went away. Wang could also have the king of hearts and respectable clubs. 7♣ required the king of hearts and strong clubs. The prospect of 7♠ was higher. Sun bid 7♠, a Queen Bid. A law of grand slam involved crucial queens. (7♣ happened to go down.)

Dummy ruffed the lead of a diamond. Sun played the king of spades, ace of hearts, and ruffed a second diamond. She led a club to the ace and drew trumps. The fifth club took care of her heart loser in hand. A trump lead would test declarer. She covered the lead in hand and ruffed a diamond in dummy. Returning to the ace of hearts, she ruffed a second diamond with the king of spades. She returned to hand with the ace of clubs to draw trumps and claimed. This required a likely 3-2 spade break gauged from the lead. If a 4-1 spade break had seemed likely, declarer would have needed to risk the ten of clubs as a third entry to hand.

2

TREASURING
YOUR QUEEN

TIPS FOR
Declarer

Q Develop skillful play surrounding the queens.
Q Confirm the need of your finesses.
Q Explore a Queen Discovery.
Q Take minifinesses for communication.
Q Create entries by a Queen Sacrifice.
Q Cross-ruff when a defender has shown strong or long trumps.
Q A camouflage with a queen requires relevant spot cards.

This chapter is for declarers. It commences with hands about unnecessary and miniskirt finesses and moves on to queen deployment, camouflage ducks, and executing a sham Queen or Jack Sacrifice. In chess, a sham Queen Sacrifice is a tactic of sacrificing your queen to win the game. "Queen promotion," or "Queening," is the chess term for advancing a pawn to the eighth rank, whereupon it is promoted to a queen—usually to decisive effect. In this book, "Queening" has a similar sense: encouraging players to win by skillful bidding and play surrounding the queens. As with all the chapters in this book, the winning play typically involves decisions surrounding the crucial queens.

A perfect painting

		♠ 96	
2005 Portugal Festival		♡ AQJ5	
Open team		◇ Q9432	
W/ Neither vulnerable		♣ J4	

♠ J52		♠ 74
♡ 97		♡ K10864
◇ AK108		◇ 75
♣ A1093		♣ Q862

	♠ AKQ1083
	♡ 32
	◇ J6
	♣ K75

West	North	East	South
1◇	Pass	1♡	1♠
Pass	1NT	Pass	2♠

Players prefer declaring and finessing. The first three hands demonstrate Queening plays. After leading the ace of diamonds, West returned the nine of hearts. All twelve declarers automatically put in the jack, thinking that eight tricks were secure. East took with his king and smartly returned a heart to the ace. Declarers knew West would ruff a queen of hearts continuation. He led a club to the king and West's ace. Defenders led trumps. Eight declarer tricks shrunk to seven for one down, minus 50.

East bid hearts. He should hold the king. The North-South shape and honour cards were perfect. Play the ace of hearts, draw trumps, and float the jack of diamonds to the ace. West was endplayed. An exit in a minor suit gave away a trick. West returned a heart to the queen and king. This endplayed East. His return presented declarer with the eighth trick. Like an adored painting, the ♡QJ, ◇QJ, and ♣KJ were all immaculately positioned. Regardless of the location of the king of hearts, refusing the finesse in hearts was a perfect response to a perfect painting.

A redundant finesse

		♠ J6	
2007 UK		♡ 86	
Lederer Memorial Trophy		◇ AK8642	
N/ Neither vulnerable		♣ AK7	

	♠ K874		♠ 53
	♡ AK10973		♡ Q54
	◇ Q3		◇ J1095
	♣ 6		♣ 10532

		♠ AQ1092	
		♡ J2	
		◇ 7	
		♣ QJ984	

West	*North*	*East*	*South*
Hallberg	Peterson	McIntosh	Short
	1NT	Pass	2♡
Double	Pass	Pass	3♣
Pass	3◇	Pass	3♠
Pass	4♠		

This hand featured another automatic finesse. Both rooms played in 4♠. In the other room, West led the ace and king of hearts, and shifted to a club. Declarer took with dummy's ace and passed the jack of spades. He lost one more spade, making 420. In this room, Hallberg sat West. He once played for Sweden, then shifted to the UK, winning the World Senior Team in 2010. He also won the Vanderbilt in 2006. After cashing two top hearts, he knew a continuation would yield a ruff and discard. There appeared to be little future in the minor suits. He persisted with a third heart.

Declarer ruffed with the jack in dummy and played a spade to his nine. West played his king and submitted a fourth heart. East ruffed with the five of spades, forcing declarer's ten. His magnificent trump spots were reduced to ♠AQ2. He lost a trick to the ♠874 in West. The solution to Hallberg's hook was deceptively simple. West showed his long hearts. East could not promote trumps by leading hearts. Provided trumps broke no worse than 4-2, there was no need for a finesse in trumps. Put the brakes on the automatic finesse; play the ace and queen of spades, and score 420.

Asymmetry

2007 BBO Internet	♠ QJ107		
IMP pairs	♡ QJ975		
E/ Neither vulnerable	◊ —		
	♣ A732		

♠ 82		♠ K6543
♡ K4		♡ 108
◊ AKQJ9873		◊ 542
♣ K		♣ 1054

	♠ A9	
	♡ A632	
	◊ 106	
	♣ QJ986	

West	North	East	South
	Clement		Chinese Taipei
		Pass	Pass
3NT	Double	Pass	4♣
Pass	4♡	Pass	6♡

Appropriate finesses can decide marginal slams. For the above deal, we were the only pair to reach a slam. I faced two bidding decisions. My double of 3NT risked a pass from partner, although we should beat it down three, plus 500. After 4♣, I needed to find our best spot. It was tempting to bid 4◊ or 5♣. My 4♡ aimed to invite further clarification. This should show both majors. My expert partner, being careful so far, showed little hesitation in bidding 6♡.

I trumped the lead of a diamond, then passed the queen of hearts to the king. West led a spade to the queen, king, and ace. My jack of hearts drew the outstanding trumps. I went to dummy with the nine of spades and led the queen of clubs, to the king and ace. I led a club and faced my third decision and fourth finesse. Where was the ten of clubs?

Deducing asymmetry, I decided to finesse. West had ♡K4 and possibly a doubleton in spades. With a doubleton in clubs and solid diamonds, an expert would unlikely open a 3NT bid. I scored 980. The contract would still make if East did not cover my queen of spades. My bidding appeared overly optimistic, requiring three of four finesses. But the optimism was built on a foundation of likely successful finesses of my queens in the major suits. That would match a normal 3NT opening. It was fortunate that my asymmetric finesses succeeded against an asymmetric 3NT opening.

A miniskirt finesse

2000 USA Fall National		♠ KQ8	
Ladies pairs		♡ J8764	
E/ Neither vulnerable		◊ AQ107	
		♣ 8	

	♠ A		♠ J103
	♡ KQ9532		♡ A
	◊ J54		◊ K82
	♣ 952		♣ AQJ1063

		♠ 976542	
		♡ 10	
		◊ 963	
		♣ K74	

West	North	East	South
Quinn		Breed	
		1♣	Pass
1♡	Double	3♣	4♠
5♣			

A finesse of a 5 over a 4 is rare. South led a heart against 5♣. Breed declared as East. (East-West have contributed to many USA wins in world women championships.) She took the lead with her ace, crossed to the ace of spades, and finessed a club to her queen and South's king. North put up her ace when South returned a diamond. If she attacked spades, dummy would have to trump and declarer would have no chance. She led a heart for a possible promotion in trumps.

Breed ruffed with her jack. She led the three of clubs to the five of clubs when South played low. The miniskirt finesse succeeded. She ruffed a heart with the ten of clubs, establishing hearts in dummy. The nine of clubs drew the outstanding trump in South. She cashed the ♡KQ9 in dummy, pitching losers in hand, scoring 400.

When declarer played the three of clubs, South must rise with the seven of clubs. The five of clubs remaining in dummy would be smaller than the lowest club (the six) in declarer. With concentration, an expert should realize the power of the hearts and the communication problem facing declarer. South saw the two, three, four, and five of clubs. The five of clubs could not be an entry if she forced out the nine. While sympathetic to South, give full marks to Breed.

Missing a U-turn

		♠ K1094	
2001 Germany		♡ —	
International Festival teams		◊ K9863	
W/ Both vulnerable		♣ 9874	

	♠ 82		♠ AQ76
	♡ QJ983		♡ AK6
	◊ Q		◊ J1072
	♣ KQ532		♣ J6

		♠ J53	
		♡ 107542	
		◊ A54	
		♣ A10	

West	*North*	*East*	*South*
Aujaleu		Adad	
Pass	Pass	1NT	Pass
2◊ (transfer)	Pass	2♡	Pass
3♣	Pass	4♡	

Finesses are usually one-way. In 4♡, most South led a small spade to the nine and queen. Declarer played a club to the king in dummy and a club to his jack, taken by the ace. South continued with the jack of spades to the ace. Declarer started trumps with the ace and king. He smoothly finessed the ten of hearts in South. When clubs failed to break, he had nine tricks for minus 100.

A 5-0 break in trumps was not unexpected. Declarer already had three tricks. An unusual play, resembling a U-turn, was a heart to the queen. Ruff a club with the ace of hearts, ruff a spade in hand, ruff another club with the king of hearts, and ruff the fourth spade. There were eight tricks. Play any side suit. With ♡J9 in hand, declarer collected two further tricks for 620.

If defenders had followed to the first heart, declarer would have led a club and ruffed with the ace. He would have cashed the king of hearts. If trumps broke 3-2, there would be no further problem. He would return to hand to draw trumps and enjoy the established clubs. If trumps broke 4-1, he would have ruffed a spade and led the good clubs. Declarer had ♡J9 and South had ♡107. The defence scored only one more trump and a diamond.

The clues were the lead of a spade by South and his drop of the ten on the first club, reflecting his shortage in the black suits. Any long trumps in a defender should lie with South. An effective strategy was the establishment of clubs using the top trumps in dummy, while retaining trump length in hand. This required leading clubs from hand. Taking the first trump with the queen was essential when South held five trumps. The natural finesse in trump was misconceived. The Queening play direction was a U-turn.

Blowing your horn

2007 BBO Internet	♠ 854		
IMP pairs	♡ 7		
N/ EW vulnerable	◇ AJ10643		
	♣ 432		

	♠ KQJ107		♠ A9
	♡ 9862		♡ KQ54
	◇ 2		◇ KQ7
	♣ AJ9		♣ Q1085

		♠ 632	
		♡ AJ103	
		◇ 985	
		♣ K76	

West	North	East	South
West	*North*	*East*	*South*
Expert	Expert	Clement	Expert
	Pass	1NT	Pass
2♣	2◇	2♡	Pass
4♡	Pass	Pass	Double

Doubling a suit contract with a balanced hand is risky. We missed the better contracts of 3NT or 4♠. South doubled 4♡, announcing his ♡AJ10 four-card in trumps. North took the lead of a small diamond with his ace and returned a diamond. I played the king and queen of diamonds, discarding two clubs in dummy. I crossed to the ace of clubs and led a heart to my king. South took with the ace and returned a spade.

I let this run to my nine and ruffed a club. A spade to my ace allowed another lead of a club. Dummy ruffed and played the king of spades. I ruffed with the four of trumps, the Grand coup. South had ♡J103. On the next lead of my fourth club, he ruffed with his jack, otherwise dummy's trump would be the ninth trick and my queen of hearts fulfilling 4♡ for 790. He returned a low heart. I put up the nine of hearts at trick 12. The queen of hearts took the last trick. My unknown partner saw the four hands and commented that he did not know how to play, let alone to make, the contract quickly. He exaggerated. Once a defender blew his horn, declarer assessed his shape and played accordingly. A Grand coup accomplished my mission.

A brighter double would be South holding good black suits and a void in hearts. This might distract declarer from the winning line, as demonstrated in several international matches in 2011.

A supernatural finesse

1997 Bermuda Bowl
Poland v Tunisia
N/ Both vulnerable

	♠ 82
	♡ K74
	◊ Q1086
	♣ Q1097

♠ AQJ53		♠ 94
♡ A83		♡ QJ652
◊ AJ542		◊ K3
♣ —		♣ J653

	♠ K1076
	♡ 109
	◊ 97
	♣ AK642

West	*North*	*East*	*South*
Romanski		Kowalski	
	Pass	Pass	1♣
1♠	Pass	1NT	Pass
3◊	Pass	3♡	Pass
4♡	Double		

This hand features several intriguing finesses. The normal lead was a club against a popular 4♡ contract. Declarer ruffed. He crossed to the king of diamonds and finessed a spade to the queen. Most declarers played the ace of diamonds and ruffed a diamond. South overruffed and led a trump. Dummy took with the ace. The following diagram showed the positions.

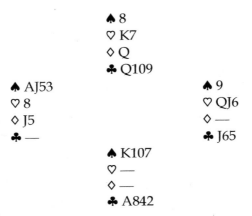

```
                    ♠ 8
                    ♡ K7
                    ◇ Q
                    ♣ Q109
      ♠ AJ53                        ♠ 9
      ♡ 8                           ♡ QJ6
      ◇ J5                          ◇ —
      ♣ —                           ♣ J65
                    ♠ K107
                    ♡ —
                    ◇ —
                    ♣ A842
```

When Zia of USA declared against France, he ruffed a diamond, ruffed a club, and played a diamond. North Perron discarded a spade. Declarer discarded a spade (or a club, with the same result). Declarer led the spade ace. North ruffed. Declarer could overruff but would have to lose two clubs and the king of hearts for down one. When Vernon of France declared, he ruffed a diamond and finessed a spade to the jack. He led the fifth diamond. If North had ruffed with the king of hearts and returned a trump, he would have beaten the contract.

Kowalski showed how to make his doubled contract. He ruffed a diamond with the jack of hearts, the Queening play. He finessed a spade to the jack, and led the fifth diamond. If North declined to ruff, declarer ruffed with the six, ruffed a club, led a spade, and scored his queen of hearts, Coup en passant. North ruffed with the king of hearts and returned a trump. Now declarer let the eight of hearts in dummy win and cashed the ace of spades, pitching a club. The queen of hearts was the tenth trick, scoring 790. Declarers missed the significance of the eight of hearts in dummy. Only Kowalski found the missing link, a supernatural self-finesse.

A supernatural scissors

2000 Poland	♠ K3
Open pairs	♡ QJ1085
E/ Neither vulnerable	◇ A43
	♣ AQ8

	♠ A4		♠ Q6
	♡ 9643		♡ A7
	◇ 2		◇ K8765
	♣ J109654		♣ K732

♠ J1098752
♡ K2
◇ QJ109
♣ —

West	*North* Lesniewski	*East*	*South* Harasimowicz
		1◇	3♠
Pass	4♠		

Beware of the Scissors coup. West led a diamond. South (Ewa Harasimowicz) instantly recognised its singleton status. She put up the ace, figuring how to prevent East from getting the lead. She had to lose two aces and the king of diamonds. A diamond ruff derailed the contract.

If East held the ace of spades, the contract would go down. Without the ace of spades, East had to hold the ace of hearts and the king of clubs for his opening bid. Declarer needed to discard two hearts to engineer her Scissors. Harasimowicz discarded a heart on the ace of clubs and played the eight of clubs.

East ducked in tempo. With the lone queen loitering in dummy, it seemed foolish to play his king. Declarer discarded her heart king. West took the naughty eight with his jack and tried a heart. Declarer ruffed, played a spade, and, according to her analysis, put up the king of spades: it held. She played a spade. She lost to the ace of spades and a diamond, making 4♠.

The supernatural Scissors denied East an entry in the ace of hearts. Even if East detected the singleton lead, covering the eight with his king seemed inhuman. Regrettably, he did not have another higher club. This hand shows off the fine art of using the queens in clubs and spades, an outstanding Queening play with a Queen Discovery of the queen of spades.

The queen sacrifice

```
2007 Netherlands              ♠ 10
Orange v 2006                 ♡ A8
   Rosenblum champions        ◊ AKJ54
W/ NS vulnerable              ♣ J9843
              ♠ J73                          ♠ A964
              ♡ KQ642                        ♡ J7
              ◊ 72                           ◊ Q963
              ♣ 752                          ♣ K106
                           ♠ KQ852
                           ♡ 10953
                           ◊ 108
                           ♣ AQ
```

West	North	East	South
Ramondt	*Helgemo*	*Westra*	*Helness*
Pass	1◊	Pass	1♠
Pass	2♣	Pass	2NT
Pass	3NT		

Donating your queen voluntarily seems illogical. In chess, a queen sacrifice is an unusual strategy to gain advantage for scoring a spectacular win. In this hand, Helness demonstrated a new dimension. Helgemo and Helness were world team champions in 2006 and 2007. Netherlands invited the 2006 squad for a friendly match.

The hand is switched 180 degrees to facilitate reading. Helness received the lead of a heart in 3NT. He ducked to the jack and took the continuation with the ace. He then led to the king of spades and surrendered the club queen, a Queen Sacrifice. Westra sat East and ducked the Greek gift. Declarer cashed the ace of clubs, crossed to dummy with the ace of diamonds, and played a third club to the king. The position was as follows.

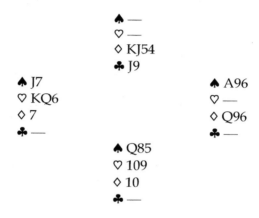

♠ —
♡ —
♦ KJ54
♣ J9

♠ J7   ♠ A96
♡ KQ6   ♡ —
♦ 7   ♦ Q96
♣ —   ♣ —

♠ Q85
♡ 109
♦ 10
♣ —

East was on lead. He had to give declarer an additional spade or diamond trick. With four clubs, the ace of hearts, the king of spades, and the ace and king of diamonds, declarer scored 600. If East took the club queen with his king and returned a club (best) to declarer's ace, declarer could duck a diamond, scoring three diamonds and four clubs.

If West held the king of clubs, the contract always went down. The Queen Sacrifice helped discover the breaks in clubs. If declarer passed the ten of diamonds—an expert—East would duck. There would be inadequate entries to enjoy the entangled clubs. In chess, the donated queen is a sham sacrifice, pinpointing that East should not take the queen. Nevertheless, Helness accomplished his mission.

A Trojan horse

2004 Australia
W/ EW vulnerable

		♠ AKJ6	
		♡ AKQ542	
		◇ —	
		♣ AQ10	
♠ Q752			♠ 103
♡ 9			♡ J108
◇ AK975			◇ QJ102
♣ K75			♣ 9862
		♠ 984	
		♡ 763	
		◇ 8643	
		♣ J43	

West	North	East	South
1◇	Double	2◇	2♡
Pass	3◇	Pass	3♡
Pass	6♡		

Donating a queen does not always work. South bid 2♡ voluntarily with three tiny cards. He landed in an ambitious slam. West led the king of diamonds. Dummy ruffed. Two rounds of trumps revealed a 3-1 break. The finesse in spades might be on, but it required an even break or a doubleton Q10 with West. The jack of clubs as an entry seemed unappealing. Defenders would duck your volunteered queen of clubs, waiting for the right time to score their king. The chance of avoiding a loser in spades was slim.

West opened. The finesse in clubs should succeed. Declarer hit upon the charm of a donated jack of spades. If swallowed, declarer would win the return, draw the remaining trump, and cash the ace of spades. When the ten of spades appeared, the nine solicited an entry to finesse the clubs. Declarer tried the jack of spades. West ducked the Trojan horse. Declarer shifted to an alternative. He did not draw trumps, but played the ace and king of spades. East ruffed the king. Declarer won the return in dummy, ruffed a spade, and led the jack of clubs through West, making the slam for 980. If East had ruffed the fourth round of spades, declarer would have won the return and led a trump to his six to perform the finesse in clubs. The jack of spades was a sham Jack Sacrifice, similar to the queen of clubs played by Helness in the previous hand. Taking or leaving the false gift of a Trojan horse didn't matter: the opponents had to surrender.

Helen of Troy

2003 NEC Cup final
UK/Argentina v Poland
E/ NS vulnerable

	♠ K98	
	♡ 9876	
	◊ J1093	
	♣ K5	
♠ Q7654		♠ AJ3
♡ 5		♡ A2
◊ AK876		◊ 542
♣ 108		♣ AJ432
	♠ 102	
	♡ KQJ1043	
	◊ Q	
	♣ Q976	

West	North	East	South
Armstrong	Lesniewski	Callagan	Martens
		1NT	Pass
2♡	Pass	2♠	Pass
3◊	Pass	3♠	Pass
3NT	Pass	4♠	

Kwiecien	Senior	Pszczola	Lambardi
		1♣	2♡
2♠	3♡	3♠	Pass
4♠			

The war fought over Helen of Troy has been the inspiration for literature and operas. The story is even echoed in this hand. In both rooms, the lead was a heart. Taking the ace in hand, declarers advanced a diamond to the queen and ace. They finessed a spade successfully to the jack and led a second diamond. South discarded a heart as the king won. The contract succeeds if South holds three trumps. Hopefully, declarers give up a third diamond to the jack. The fourth diamond from North promoted a second trump trick for the defence. Declarers scored minus 50 in both rooms. Poland squandered more than 40 IMPs in the last session, losing by an IMP.

Learning from the legend of Troy helped declarers. Ducking the diamond queen, declarer took the next trick and ruffed a heart. He finessed a spade to the jack, cashed the ace of spades, played the ace and king of diamonds, and ruffed a fourth diamond with East's third spade for 420. The queening play escaped two finalists. The queen of diamonds was a Helen of Troy: best to let her stay where she belonged.

Unreachable sky

		♠ 54	
2008 USA Fall National		♡ K103	
Side game		◊ J10972	
E/ Neither vulnerable		♣ 763	

♠ A82			♠ Q1093
♡ J972			♡ A64
◊ K853			◊ 64
♣ J4			♣ 10982

	♠ KJ76	
	♡ Q85	
	◊ AQ	
	♣ AKQ5	

West	North	East	South
Kantar	R Lee	Alder	L Lee
		Pass	2NT
Pass	3NT		

We continue with the Queen Sacrifice. West led a small heart against 3NT. East took with his ace and attacked spades with the nine, promising zero or two honours. West took declarer's jack with the ace and returned the eight. Declarer ducked and took the continuation of a spade with her king.

Declarer unblocked diamonds, playing the ace and queen. When West ducked, she led a heart up. Kantar sat West. He inserted the jack, forcing the king. Had West played small, declarer would have inserted the ten. She would then have two entries in dummy to force out the king of diamonds and to enjoy the diamonds. As it was, declarer had eight tricks for minus 50. Declarer should have donated her queen on the ace of hearts at trick one.

There was an elegant solution after the failure to unblock the fatal queen. Before playing a heart up, declarer cashed her ♣AKQ. West inserted his jack of hearts as before. After taking the jack with the king, declarer led the jack of diamonds, dispatching the queen of hearts. West was endplayed, having only hearts and diamonds left. The unreachable dummy was now reachable.

There was an elegant counter. When declarer ducked the eight of spades at the third trick, West should have returned a heart, taking out a premature entry from dummy. Alternatively, East could have played back a heart at trick two or refused to win the ace of hearts at trick one. This alternative might have been double dummy, as declarer could have three diamonds or weaker spades.

An American duck

```
1997 Bermuda Bowl        ♠ K753
USA v Norway             ♡ K8
E/ Neither vulnerable    ◇ KJ974
                         ♣ 32
        ♠ 104                         ♠ A98
        ♡ Q3                          ♡ J10652
        ◇ 5                           ◇ A102
        ♣ AJ1097654                   ♣ K8
                         ♠ QJ62
                         ♡ A974
                         ◇ Q863
                         ♣ Q
```

West	North	East	South
West	*North*	*East*	*South*
Meckstroth	Helness	Rodwell	Helgemo

[East opened and North-South competed. West declared 5♣.]

USA beat Norway, but was overwhelmed by France in the final. The two pairs at this table were well known. The older managed a coup against the younger in this deal. Declarer showed a new dimension of the Queening play.

There was no report on the exact bidding. West showed a long suit in clubs. North-South showed strength in spades and diamonds. North led a diamond. Meckstroth declared and ducked in dummy. South won with his queen and innately continued a diamond to the ace. Declarer discarded a heart. A heart was led towards the lonely queen. North won with his king and attacked spades. Rising with the ace, declarer advanced the jack of hearts. South covered and declarer ruffed. The ace and king of clubs took care of the defensive trumps. The ten of hearts discarded a losing spade, making 400.

If South rose with the ace on the first round of hearts, declarer guessed and ruffed the second heart, dropping the king. Declarer was not tested. The real test was the first trick. Seeing the vulnerability of his spades when hearts were led, declarer found a way to avoid a loser in spades by manufacturing a defensive slip. It was a far-sighted use of one's concealed queen. While South should have recognised the futility of continuing diamonds, the American duck of a sham Ace Sacrifice was too tempting for the younger Norwegian.

Queen camouflage 1993

1993 Hong Kong
Chinese Club open pairs
S/ Neither vulnerable

```
                    ♠ Q3
                    ♡ A75
                    ◇ Q97
                    ♣ KQ643
         ♠ KJ9                      ♠ 108652
         ♡ 1082                     ♡ Q9
         ◇ K104                     ◇ AJ32
         ♣ AJ82                     ♣ 105
                    ♠ A74
                    ♡ KJ643
                    ◇ 865
                    ♣ 97
```

West	North	East	South
Clement			
			Pass
1♣ (2+)	Pass	1♠	Pass
1NT			

The best of Hong Kong competed for a prestigious trophy. Scoring was match points. We missed a par contract of 2♠. Thinking I was short in clubs, North led a small club to my jack. If I worked on diamonds or spades, I needed a Queen Discovery in these two suits. Communication to dummy was problematic. Even if I guessed the queens, it was near certain that defenders would switch to hearts. I felt that we were not in a rosy contract. Remembered my Bols Tip, I tried a variation and, with little hesitation, a heart to dummy's queen, a Helen of Troy.

South won with his king and returned a club. I played small and North won with the queen. Counting my high-card points in hearts, North thought it a good idea to venture the queen of spades. I won with my king and played the nine, and played a third round, forcing out the ace. North discarded a heart fatally. I scored 150 for a top. While there was an element of luck in my camouflage, the spot cards in my hearts were the important basis for inspiring my Queening play. South thought I had ♡A10 fourth. North thought I had ♡J10 or J8 fourth. Neither would have liked to open a second round of hearts. In chess, the queen of hearts would have constituted a real Queen Sacrifice. When opponents failed to cope, it was transformed into a sham Queen Sacrifice.

I once made 6NT, missing the top diamonds. At the third trick, I led a diamond towards my concealed QJ10 fifth. I played the queen, and my left-hand opponent ducked. He held the ace and thought I was testing a long suit headed by KQ10. My right-hand opponent held the king. The queen was the twelfth trick.

Queen camouflage 2001

West	North	East	South

2001 Bermuda Bowl — ♠ 92
Italy v France — ♡ A532
S/ Both vulnerable — ◊ J10
— ♣ J9853

```
                ♠ 1086                              ♠ AK54
                ♡ 1086                              ♡ Q7
                ◊ Q642                              ◊ A973
                ♣ A62                               ♣ KQ7
                         ♠ QJ73
                         ♡ KJ94
                         ◊ K85
                         ♣ 104
```

West	North	East	South
Duboin	*Multon*	*Bocchi*	*Quantin*
			Pass
Pass	Pass	2♣ (strong)	Pass
2♡ (2 controls)	Pass	2NT	Pass
3NT			

In 1993, I played 1NT and led a heart to dummy's queen, having ♡1082 in my hand and ♡Q9 in dummy. Defenders never played that suit again. This hand occurred in 2001. 3NT failed at all other tables. The defenders always found their winning hearts.

Fast-forward eight years. South led a low spade. Declarer Bocchi guessed and put up the ten, which held. If declarer guessed diamonds, he would score three tricks, fulfilling the contract. The caveat was that he had to yield a diamond trick to a defender in between. The obvious shift to hearts signified a defeat. It did not require Smith or similar attitude signals.

Bocchi must have studied psychology. He attacked his weakest suit and led a small heart to his queen and the king. South continued with the queen of spades to the king. Bocchi led a diamond, guessing correctly by inserting the queen in dummy.

The ace of diamonds and a diamond came next. Collecting his king, South insisted with the jack of spades. Declarer scored 600. Seeing a play identical to mine succeed in a world championship eight years later was a rare treat.

Queen camouflage 2010

2010 Australia	♠ 103	
Rubber bridge	♡ 64	
N/ Neither vulnerable	◇ AQ10875	
	♣ 532	

♠ A98652		♠ J7
♡ J107		♡ AK853
◇ 3		◇ K64
♣ Q76		♣ J104

	♠ KQ4	
	♡ Q92	
	◇ J92	
	♣ AK98	

It took nine years for me to read about another real Queen Sacrifice in declarer play. North opened 3◇ and Courtney responded 3NT. On the lead of the six of spades, he guessed to put up dummy's ten to the jack and king. He passed the jack of diamonds to the king. Before returning a spade, East tried the king of hearts, requesting partner to drop his highest card. Seeing partner's jack and declarer's two, he continued with the ace. Courtney dropped the queen of hearts, and West the ten. West thought that East had AK9 sixth in hearts, and East thought West held J1097. Their spirits were high, smelling victory.

East continued a small heart to the magical nine in his partner, and waited patiently for more heart winners. The nine surfaced, but it was with Courtney. He made just nine tricks. Courtney was awarded the IBPA 2010 best declarer play. Had Courtney guessed the spade and heart positions on the first trick, he would not have sacrificed his queen of hearts and would have deprived himself of an unforgettable bridge ecstasy.

3
A GOLDEN OPENING

TIPS FOR
Leads and Responses

Q   Develop skillful play surrounding the queens.

Q   Consider an opening Queen Lead.

Q   Consider a Queen Lead for entries in partner.

Q   Consider a Queen Lead or underlead when endplayed.

Q   Lead a short major against 3NT with a weak hand.

Q   Lead a small trump from a doubleton queen.

Q   Replace the principle of restricted choice with your own choice.

Q   Defeat a Dentist coup with a Queen Lead.

Q   Defeat a Bath coup or suit establishment with a Queen Duck.

Q   Examine your third-best when making fourth-best leads.

Q   Avoid revealing singleton leads.

T he response to an opening lead is as important as the lead. An often-ignored area is exit cards in mid-defence. This chapter discusses these subjects with hands featuring queens. Examples are leading the queen with three cards or with AQ of a suit, ducking an opening lead holding a suit with touching honours of KQ or QJ, blocking fourth-best leads, doubleton honour trump leads, and a singleton lead that gave the show away.

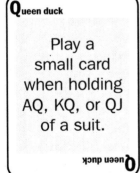

Queen duck

Play a small card when holding AQ, KQ, or QJ of a suit.

Queen duck

Queen lead

Lead a queen unnaturally when holding AQ, Q, third, or similar.

Queen lead

Queen underlead

Lead small unnaturally when holding AQ, KQ, or QJ of a suit.

Queen underlead

Queening your lead

		♠ 53	
1997 USA		♡ 9876	
Cavendish pairs		◇ AJ964	
E/ EW vulnerable		♣ 102	

♠ J2			♠ A1084
♡ KQ53			♡ A2
◇ K752			◇ 3
♣ KJ9			♣ A76543

		♠ KQ976	
		♡ J104	
		◇ Q108	
		♣ Q8	

West	*North*	*East*	*South*
Helgemo	Ekeblad	Helness	Sukoneck
		1♣	1♠
Double	Pass (no top ♠) 2♣		Pass
2♠	Pass	2NT	Pass
3NT			

We began with an unconventional lead. The occasion was a tournament with cash prizes. Its distinct feature was a cash pool for players and a larger cash pool for bidders. Players bid for the winning pairs in an auction. You could lose heavily in the tournament but reward yourself by predicting the winners, and vice versa.

Sukoneck was South. By his pass of 1♠ doubled, North showed no top spade or support. The bidding suggested a red-suit lead, but West showed a heart suit and stoppers in diamonds. The shaky clubs in South were ripe for reaping by declarer. Defenders needed to take five tricks before declarer took nine. South made the Queen Lead of a diamond. He was on target, scoring 100. This was an old tactic described in the 1993 Bols Tip. A partnership should, however, be aware that the lead of the queen of diamonds did not promise a doubleton or the jack.

Queen identity

		♠ AK432	
2008 USA		♡ 109	
Reisinger board a match teams		◇ 982	
W/ NS vulnerable		♣ A64	

♠ 10875		♠ Q96
♡ KQ7		♡ J82
◇ A64		◇ KJ7
♣ 973		♣ K1085

	♠ J	
	♡ A6543	
	◇ Q1053	
	♣ QJ2	

West	*North*	*East*	*South*
Weinstein		Garner	
Pass	1♠	Pass	1NT

Queens have different meanings for different partnerships. In the other room, South declared the same 1NT contract. West led the queen of hearts. East encouraged. Declarer ducked twice and took the third round. The queen of clubs lost to the king. Declarer had two spades, three hearts, and two clubs. He scored 120 after a mix-up in the defence.

In this room, 1NT was semiforcing. Opener passed with a minimum and a flat hand. Weinstein as West made the same lead. The ten and nine in dummy alerted Garner that the queen of hearts should be from ♡KQx. With a four-card suit, West would have led a small one. With strength, West led the king, asking East to unblock his highest card. Garner therefore discouraged. West switched to a spade, dummy ducked to the queen. East returned the five of clubs to the queen. Declarer floated a small heart. Other alternatives did not fare better.

West put up his king and returned a club to the king. East continued clubs to knock out the ace. Declarer tried a diamond.

East put up his king to cash the fourth club. East exited a heart. Declarer could take his three heart tricks, but had to lead diamonds, losing the last two tricks for minus 200. Declarer could not fare better by cashing the ace and king of spades in dummy. He had to discard a winner in hearts and a diamond, arriving at the same result. Once East explored the queen of hearts identity, declarer had no suitable encounter.

Trapping a king

2003 USA		♠ K87	
Open team trials		♡ 5	
N/ Both vulnerable		◊ AQ963	
		♣ K632	

♠ J3	♠ A106
♡ 1032	♡ J9876
◊ K104	◊ 52
♣ AQ985	♣ J104

	♠ Q9542
	♡ AKQ4
	◊ J87
	♣ 7

West	*North*	*East*	*South*
Compton	Weichsel		Sontag
	1◊	Pass	1♠
Pass	2♣	Pass	2◊ (game force)
Pass	3♠ (short♡+3♠)	Pass	4♠

This hand shows off a remarkable Queen Lead. Compton as West knew dummy was 3-1-5-4. His ◊K10 and ♣AQ awaited an uncertain destiny. A lead from a major suit was not promising. He fancied the queen of clubs as the lead, preserving his good clubs while hoping to trap a king.

Declarer, a world champion, thought it blameless to duck in dummy. Dummy ducked the second club. Declarer ruffed in hand. He led to the king of spades, taken by East with the ace. East returned the jack of clubs. Declarer discarded a diamond, expecting West to ruff from three trumps, thereby wasting a natural winner. The appearance of the ace of clubs was uncompromising. The subsequent loss of a trump sunk an impregnable contract. Because of the fortunate positions in the diamonds and clubs, declarer should lose two spades and one club. Compton reversed the fortune. It was not a lucky lead, but a Queening lead.

A princely jack

2004 USA	♠ 73		
Grand National teams	♡ 102		
S/ Neither vulnerable	◇ K10753		
	♣ K862		

West		East
♠ AQ96		♠ J1052
♡ A53		♡ Q6
◇ 94		◇ J82
♣ A1073		♣ QJ94

♠ K84
♡ KJ9874
◇ AQ6
♣ 5

West	North	East	South
			Shenkin
			1♡
1♠	Double	3♠	4♡

Being endplayed early is not amusing. The double by North showed minors. Declaring 4♡, Shenkin decided to win the diamond lead with his queen, cashed his ace of diamonds, and led a club. His Dentist coup to endplay West worked. Winning his ace of clubs, West elected to return a club. The king provided a discard of a spade in hand, and an entry for finessing a trump by passing the ten. West won with the ace and continued a club, ruffed by declarer. The king of hearts dropped the queen for 450. Shenkin won the event with his team.

A Queen Sacrifice was the recipe. A normal count signal by East on the first club should reveal declarer's singleton. A return of a club yielded a trick and an entry to dummy. Adopting the concept of Queen Lead, West played the queen of spades. It was not desperado. East supported spades and might hold a princely jack. The Queen Lead lost to the king of spades, but declarer had no suitable return. He tried a spade. East won with his jack and returned a diamond for down one, plus 50.

An impossible dream

1999 USA	♠ K109		
Cavendish pairs	♡ A653		
E/ NS vulnerable	◇ K752		
	♣ K2		

♠ 7654		♠ AQ3	
♡ Q872		♡ 9	
◇ J		◇ 84	
♣ J973		♣ AQ108654	

	♠ J82		
	♡ KJ104		
	◇ AQ10963		
	♣ —		

West	North	East	South
Weichsel	Moss	Sontag	Gitelman
		2♣	2◇
4♣	5◇		

A crucial queen determined this hand. Both pairs were world champions. North-South won the Rosenblum Cup in 2010.

Many pairs made 3NT or 4♡. The competitive bidding ended in 5◊.

West led a heart which ran to the ten in declarer. Gitelman drew trumps and ruffed a small club. He cashed the ace of hearts, noting the discard from East. He played the king of clubs, pitching a spade. East took his ace of clubs. Endplayed, he played the ace of spades and a spade, hoping partner held the jack. This was an impossible dream. Declarer took the spade with his jack. The king of spades in dummy parked a losing heart. If East returned a club, declarer would discard another spade as dummy ruffed. Declarer endplayed East with a spade. A spade gave away a trick. A club yielded another ruff and discard.

Advising East to return the three of spade after his ace of clubs invited ridicule and scorn, but this was the only winning return. Declarer had to lose a heart and a spade in addition to the club. The intact ♠AQ in East guarded the ♠K10 in dummy and the ♠J in declarer. The spade three gave away a trick. The other options gave away two. Giving more thought, the three was not an impossible dream, but an impossible return turned possible: a Queen Underlead.

A possible dream

	♠ AJ8643	
2000 Netherlands	♡ 8	
National Team semifinal	♦ A54	
N/ NS vulnerable	♣ K72	

♠ 75		♠ KQ2
♡ KQJ106		♡ 743
♦ J106		♦ 83
♣ J103		♣ AQ654

	♠ 109	
	♡ A952	
	♦ KQ972	
	♣ 98	

West	*North*	*East*	*South*
Jansma	Eskes	Verhees	Von Seida
	1♠	Pass	1NT
Pass	2♠ (6+ card)	Pass	3♠
Pass	4♠		

A major tenace is the AQ of a suit. This was another challenge for a defender holding a major tenace. A part-score was played in the other room. In this room, Verhees sat East. He led a heart against 4♠, to dummy's ace. A spade was led to his queen. Verhees did an accounting. Declarer had ten tricks with the ace of hearts, four trumps, and five diamonds with the ace. He had three tricks in ♠KQ and ♣A. He needed one more. Verhees discovered a Queen Sacrifice, and led the queen of clubs.

Declarer could cash the ace of spades and run diamonds. Ruffing the third round, the defence would score two club tricks for down one. Instead, declarer crossed to dummy in diamonds to repeat the finesse in spades. East won, returned a club to partner's lovely jack, and set the contract with his ace of clubs. If declarer had a 6-2-3-2 or 6-2-2-3 shape, East would still defeat the contract.

The key card was the jack of clubs. The ten was surplus. The caveat was that a small club from East would not work if declarer held the ten. Declarer took the jack with his king and played the ten. On winning with his honour, East could not lead trumps without losing his king. He needed to let partner win the second club to lead a trump. The Queen Lead from a major tenace performed the magic, once again.

Maximisation

2008 NEC Cup
Israel v Canada
N/ Both vulnerable

North hand:
♠ AQJ872
♡ Q
◇ K85
♣ J32

West hand:
♠ K6
♡ A86
◇ AJ942
♣ AQ6

East hand:
♠ 543
♡ J10974
◇ Q76
♣ 85

South hand:
♠ 109
♡ K532
◇ 103
♣ K10974

West	North	East	South
Barel	N Gartaganis	Campanile	J Gartaganis
	1♠	Pass	1NT
Pass	2♠ (6-card)		

A defender can mitigate his damages when endplayed. Campanile was one of Israel's best. She sat East and led a club. West took his ace and queen, and led a third club. She ruffed. Endplayed, she assessed declarer's shape. Declarer showed six spades and three clubs. If he had three diamonds, a heart lead would be futile, as declarer should have at least a queen. A diamond yielded a crucial finesse for declarer. A trump might trap an honour held by partner, but it cut down the ruffing potential of dummy and the entry for clubs. It maximised defence prospects.

Barel complimented Campanile's good return by ducking the nine of spades; otherwise, the ten in dummy was an entry to cash the good clubs. Declarer could draw trumps, or lead a heart, or lead a diamond for his seventh trick. Whichever way, defenders could prevent him from reaching dummy again to make his contract. While returning a trump presented a free finesse, declarer's joy quickly evaporated.

An honourable king

1998 Generali Masters
Individuals
E/ EW vulnerable

	♠ J6	
	♡ AJ1083	
	◊ Q62	
	♣ KJ8	
♠ 5432		♠ KQ1087
♡ Q5		♡ K962
◊ J		◊ K97
♣ 1097532		♣ A
	♠ A9	
	♡ 74	
	◊ A108543	
	♣ Q64	

West	North	East	South
Kholmeev	Chemla	Helgemo	Freeman
		1♠	2◊
Pass	2♡	Pass	3◊
3♠	4◊		

The Deschapelles coup, named after a chess and whist player from the time of the French Revolution, is normally a King Sacrifice to create entries for partner. In this popular 4◊ contract, most declarers played back a spade after taking the lead with the ace of spades. On a suit return, declarer had one entry to play the queen of diamonds through East. Defence and play varied, but most declarers scored down one, losing a trick in each suit.

The eventual winner, Helgemo, sat East. He took the second spade, cashed the ace of clubs, and sailed the honourable king of hearts, Deschapelles. Dummy's ace took the trick. Declarer passed the queen of diamonds, covered by the king and ace. Declarer tried to reach dummy via a club to take the marked finesse of the nine of diamonds. Helgemo spoiled the plan by ruffing. He led a heart to the queen and ruffed the return of another club. The sham King Sacrifice succeeded. Down two was almost a top score. If declarer respected the 3♠ bid by West, he might suspect the King Sacrifice. Cashing the ace of clubs facing KJ in dummy aroused suspicion. He should have played the ten of trumps, conceding down one for a modest score.

A humiliated king

	♠ A103		
2008 Olympiad	♡ J109542		
Norway v Egypt	◇ 85		
E/ Both vulnerable	♣ 109		

♠ K98752		♠ Q4
♡ A		♡ Q876
◇ 943		◇ AQ10
♣ A84		♣ KJ75

	♠ J6	
	♡ K3	
	◇ KJ762	
	♣ Q632	

West	North	East	South
El-Ahmadi	Helness	Sadek	Helgemo
		1♣	1◇
1♠	Pass	1NT	Pass
2◇	Pass	3NT	

Leading the king from a doubleton was not new. When UK played Australia, West bid 1♡ over 1◇, a transfer to spades. North doubled, showing hearts. South led the king of hearts against Australia's 3NT. Defenders could establish the hearts, defeating the contract. Good card reading might allow 4♠ to make.

Helgemo once led an unsupported king from four-card in mid-defence, creating an entry to his partner (not Helness) via the queen. For the hand shown here, Helgemo led the king of hearts without the slightest hesitation. It was the only lead to defeat the contract. Declarer won with his ace and played a spade. Helness philosophized. This could be the ninth trick for declarer, five clubs with KQ in hand, AK of diamonds, one heart and one spade. The arithmetic of high-card points would be 14, matching the bids of the declarer.

As North had not shown any preference in hearts, he presumed South to hold the queen. He rose with his ace of spades and returned a heart. Declarer took the rest of the tricks by locating the queen of clubs and a squeeze. The failed ♡K lead became a real King Sacrifice. This time misinterpretation undermined Helgemo's brilliant leads. That did not discourage Helgemo or Helness.

A foolish lead

2007 Bermuda Bowl final		♠ 87	
Norway v USA		♡ KJ3	
E/ Neither vulnerable		◊ Q1063	
		♣ KQ75	

♠ KJ6		♠ 432	
♡ 98652		♡ Q4	
◊ K75		◊ 92	
♣ A2		♣ J109843	

♠ AQ1095	
♡ A107	
◊ AJ84	
♣ 6	

West	*North*	*East*	*South*
Brogeland	Garner	Saelensminde	Weinstein
		Pass	1♠
Pass	1NT	Pass	2♣ (could be strong)
Pass	2◊	Pass	2♡ (3-card)
Pass	3NT		
Zia	Helness	Rosenberg	Helgemo
		Pass	1♠
Pass	1NT	Pass	2◊
Pass	3◊	Pass	3♡
Pass	3NT	Pass	Pass
Double	Redouble		

A double of 3NT often demands a lead of dummy's first-bid suit. Brogeland, in the first room, did not fancy a double. His partner, Saelensminde, led the queen of hearts, seemingly foolishly. But a short-suit lead is the recommended strategy with a weak hand. Declarer won with his king and passed the ten of diamonds to the king. West continued hearts to the jack. Declarer passed a spade to the queen and king. The third heart exhausted the last heart stopper. Declarer could make his contract by guessing at the fourth trick that West held ♣Ax. This was antipercentage. He cashed two diamonds and finessed a spade to the ten. West won with the jack and cashed two hearts and the ace of clubs for down two, minus 100.

The refrain from doubling and the lead from a short major were expert decisions. West had four entries to establish his paltry hearts. In the other room, Zia counted four defensive tricks. His 1993 Bols Tip of the Panther Double advised defenders to double boldly, sometimes to puzzle declarer. He thought this was an appropriate occasion, also securing a spade lead. Helness had a maximum 1NT and redoubled.

Rosenberg led a spade compliantly. West covered the ten with his jack and played a small club. Helness played his king and advanced the queen of diamonds, ducked by West. Declarer led the ten of diamonds, overtook with dummy's ace, confident that West had the king. After the ace and queen of spades, West took his king and was endplayed. He could cash his minor suit winners. Declarer had the rest for 800 and 14 IMPs. By outgunning USA2, Norway was crowned world champion for the first time.

A disturbing lead

2001 USA Fall National	♠ KJ643		
Spingold knock-out team	♡ AK93		
S/ EW vulnerable	◇ Q9		
	♣ 74		

♠ Q2		♠ 875
♡ 10752		♡ 864
◇ A83		◇ KJ72
♣ A862		♣ J105

	♠ A109		
	♡ QJ		
	◇ 10654		
	♣ KQ93		

West	North	East	South
Aa	Petrunin	Groetheim	Gromov
			1NT (weak)
Pass	2♡ (transfer)	Pass	2♠
Pass	3♡	Pass	4♠

From experience, I consider the principle of restricted choice flawed. In the 2011 European Open Championship, West led a low trump against 7♠ from a doubleton. East played the queen of spades. Declarer played the ace of spades. Dummy had ♠K10 fifth. Declarer next finessed a trump to the ten of spades, a restricted choice. East had doubleton ♠QJ for down one. The restricted choice was based on the probability that East would play the jack or queen half of the time if he had two honours, and all the time if he held a singleton honour. However, West would always play low-high with his small cards, holding two or three cards. Declarer fared better by assessing a 2-2 or 3-1 break.

Gromov declared 4♠ as South. He took the lead of a small trump with the nine. Unsure of its status, he led a diamond to the nine and jack. East returned a club, covered by the king and ace. West cashed his ace of diamonds and led a diamond, ruffed in dummy. South thought that as West had two aces in the minors and hearts had been bid, it was reasonable for Aa to lead a singleton or doubleton in spades.

Judging that West did not hold the queen and guarding against four trumps in East, declarer played a spade to his ten. The queen defeated the contract. Leading small with a doubleton or a doubleton queen was an old ploy. It defeated 4♠ at this table, and 7♠ in 2011.

An impossible singleton

2000 Olympiad final
Italy v Poland
W/ EW vulnerable

	♠ A2	
	♡ AK96	
	◊ Q952	
	♣ KJ6	
♠ Q863		♠ KJ105
♡ J2		♡ Q3
◊ 643		◊ A1087
♣ 8752		♣ A93
	♠ 974	
	♡ 108754	
	◊ KJ	
	♣ Q104	

West	North	East	South
Jassem	Lauria	Tuszynski	Versace
Pass	1NT	Pass	2◊ (♡)
Pass	2NT (accept)	Pass	3◊ (transfer)
Pass	3♡	Pass	3NT
Pass	4♡		

We continue with the lead of a trump. In the other room, Poland's Balicki as North bid 1NT and Zmudzinski passed. After a diamond lead, declarer scored nine tricks.

In this room, Italy deployed transfer bids. 2NT permitted responder a marionette response: to show support or denial.

Against 4♡, East had difficulties finding an attractive opening
lead. Tuszynski tried a small trump from his doubleton queen,
the only lead to disturb declarer. Lauria took West's jack with his
ace. He played a diamond to the king and led a heart to his king,
dropping the queen and making the contract. It was less difficult
for declarer to solve the puzzle with four missing trumps. An expert, East, having viewed the bidding, would unlikely choose a
singleton trump as his lead. There were also slim prospects of
pitching two spade losers from dummy on the diamonds. Italy
won the final.

A dauntless assumption

2002 McConnell cup   ♠ KQ8743
N/ EW vulnerable   ♡ 963
                        ◊ Q6
                        ♣ 93

         ♠ J92   ♠ 1065
         ♡ J7   ♡ AK5
         ◊ AJ842   ◊ 7
         ♣ 864   ♣ AKQJ105

                     ♠ A
                     ♡ Q10842
                     ◊ K10953
                     ♣ 72

West	North	East	South
	2♠	3♠ (ask 3NT)	Pass
5♣			

      The conventional lead with KQ sixth was the king against
a suit contract. West knew her jack did not serve as a spade stopper. She knew East must have a solid club suit. An aggressive 5♣
placed the opening lead to North, who chose a club. Declarer
played ace and king of clubs, ace of diamonds, and ruffed a dia-

mond, noting the queen from North. As South appeared to hold a
singleton spade and also the missing red-suit honours, declarer
cleverly played a small spade. South was endplayed. A heart allowed the jack to win, and a losing spade pitched on the top
hearts. A diamond allowed the jack to win for a discard of a
spade in dummy. West lost only two spades, making her contract.

A random heart lead set the contract. A dauntless lead
was a small spade. South won her ace and made a safe return.
There was no endplay. The Queen Underlead of a small spade by
North was reasonable after opponents denied a stopper. It unblocked the singleton ace of spades.

A duck in the mirror

2009 Netherlands	♠ 108752		
White House mixed teams	♡ AK9		
S/ EW vulnerable	◊ AJ7		
	♣ 83		

	♠ A9		♠ K43
	♡ J8		♡ Q7532
	◊ KQ854		◊ 93
	♣ Q1072		♣ 954

	♠ QJ6	
	♡ 1064	
	◊ 1062	
	♣ AKJ6	

West	North	East	South
Gromoeller	Zmudzinski		Seamon-Molson
			Pass
1◊	Double	Pass	2◊
Pass	2♠	Pass	3♣
Pass	3NT		

This involved a defence suit headed by KQ. 4♠ in the other room stood no chance. After the lead of a diamond, declarer suffered a diamond ruff, losing two spades, one heart, and one diamond for down two. In this room, Zmudzinski treated his two majors equally with a take-out double. This led to a 3NT contract declared by him. East led the nine of diamonds to the queen. Declarer ducked and took the diamond continuation with his jack, the Bath coup. Declarer advanced a spade towards dummy. Even if East put up her king, she had no diamond to return. Declarer took three spades and two tricks each in the other suits, making 3NT.

The play was straightforward if West was on lead. He would lead a small card. The defence was a duck in the mirror—duck the diamond lead. On the first spade, East put up her king to deliver her remaining diamond. West forced out the ace. His ace of spades was an entry for three tricks in diamonds. West could judge from the doubleton lead that declarer held ◊AJx. His ◊KQ should await a second round to knock out the ace. The mirrored duck is defined as a Queen Duck in this book. It defeated a Bath coup.

A vulnerable duck

		♠ 76	
2002 USA		♡ A973	
Open trials final		◊ A109872	
S/ Neither vulnerable		♣ J	

♠ Q98532			♠ KJ
♡ 108			♡ K64
◊ 3			◊ QJ54
♣ AQ109			♣ 8654

		♠ A104	
		♡ QJ52	
		◊ K6	
		♣ K732	

West	*North*	*East*	*South*
Rodwell	Rosenberg	Meckstroth	Zia
			1♣
1♠	Double	Redouble	2♡
2♠	4♡		

Schwartz	Nickell	Becker	Freeman
			1♣
2♠	Double	3♠	4♡

Defend carefully with a suit headed by QJ. In the second room, West led a diamond to the jack and king. Declarer led a heart to the ace and a heart to his queen, East ducking. Declarer crossed to the ace of diamonds and passed the ten of diamonds for a ruffing finesse. After ruffing East's diamond queen, he played a trump. Dummy still had a trump to enjoy the diamonds. Declarer lost one trick each of spades, hearts, and clubs to make his contract. East could have taken his king on the second trump and attacked clubs. If West took his queen and ace of clubs, dummy discarded a spade. If West took his queen of clubs and returned a small club, declarer ran to his king of clubs. Alternatively, declarer could unblock his queen of hearts on the second trump. Declarer always succeeded on the lie of the cards by establishing diamonds.

In the first room, Meckstroth articulated a Queening defence, the Queen Duck. On the lead of a diamond, he nonchalantly ducked and declarer won with the tiny six. To establish diamonds, declarer had little choice but to play the king next, ruffed by West. West returned a spade to the ace. Declarer had to lose a spade, a heart and a club for down one. To avoid the ruff, declarer could draw two rounds of trumps as in the second room. The blockage by his king of diamonds and the lack of entries in dummy prevented the establishment of diamonds. Meckstroth's diamonds were familiar faces vulnerable to being washed out by a ruffing finesse. He expected partner to have winners for his vulnerable overcalls, and the diamonds were main sources of tricks for declarer. The American duck conserved his vulnerable suit and cost declarer his contract.

A righteous lead

2006 NEC Cup	♠ 72		
Italy v Japan	♡ 108654		
S/ NS vulnerable	◊ J		
	♣ A6532		

♠ 10963		♠ AQ85
♡ KQ2		♡ J3
◊ A10762		◊ K954
♣ 8		♣ KJ10

	♠ KJ4
	♡ A97
	◊ Q83
	♣ Q974

West	*North*	*East*	*South*
Shimizu	Madala	Nakamura	Ferraro
			1♣
1◊	Double	1♡ (♠)	Pass
2♠	3♣	4♠	

Duboin	Furuta	Bocchi	Chen
			1♣
1◊	3♣	3NT	

Leading fourth best is an undeniable human right. In the first room, East-West found its fit to play 4♠. The fashionable transfer ironically placed North on lead. North happened to possess a singleton diamond. Declarer responded intelligently by taking the lead and played ace and queen of trumps. His operation succeeded in preventing a ruff in diamonds, but the positions in spades and two defensive aces doomed the contract.

In the other room, Furuta's preemptive 3♣ influenced Bocchi to declare 3NT. Playing fourth-best lead, Japan's Chen led the four of clubs. North won with the ace and returned a club to the jack and queen. South played the nine of clubs to the king.

Declarer played the king of diamonds and a small diamond to the ten, and led hearts, forcing out the ace. South now discovered that the seven blocked the clubs, and might apologize for not having shed it on the lead, an old bridge tip for leading the third highest when it is the seven or eight. An expert should recognize an unblocking third-best lead, a deviation from the fourth best, when examining his spot cards. By a smile of fortune, an adventurous 3NT scored a swing against a cultured 4♠.

Clashing your own aces

2001 Poland   ♠ 73
N/ EW vulnerable   ♡ J103
                                      ◇ KJ109732
                                      ♣ 6

♠ AQ10985   ♠ KJ
♡ —   ♡ AK7652
◇ A4   ◇ Q6
♣ AQ432   ♣ 875

                      ♠ 642
                      ♡ Q984
                      ◇ 85
                      ♣ KJ109

West	North	East	South
Lokeberg			
	3◇	3♡	Pass
3♠	Pass	4♠	Pass
4NT	Pass	5♡	Pass
5NT	Pass	6♡*	Pass
6♠			

*No minor suit king

Singleton leads against slams are seductive; singleton leads of trumps against slams are taboo. In this aggressive 6♠

contract, declarer had eleven tricks after the impressive lead of a singleton club. Declarer won the lead with his queen. He knew that North would ruff a second club. Winning tricks by ruffing clubs in dummy was not feasible. An establishment in hearts required meticulous planning. Lokeberg led a spade to the jack. He crashed his ace of diamonds on the ace of hearts, an Ace Sacrifice—and a stroke of genius. It was an Emperor's coup, named by Le Dentu.

Declarer ruffed a heart in hand, played a spade to dummy's king, and ruffed another heart. He drew trumps, cashed the ace of clubs, and played a diamond. North won with his king. With only diamonds left, he reluctantly surrendered a diamond to the queen in dummy. The hearts provided two further tricks. He scored six spades, three hearts, one diamond, and two clubs, for 1430.

The asking bid of 5NT pinpointed that declarer held all the aces and was looking for a king in the minors for a grand slam. A club lead was risky, presenting a possible finesse through partner. Declarer could succeed with a lead in the majors. He adopted a similar line but had to gauge North's shape. The otiose singleton lead gave the show away.

4

A Ruffing
Master Plan

Tips for
Ruffing and Forcing Defence

- Q Organise a ruffing plan.
- Q Avoid ruffs with natural winners.
- Q Pay attention to long side suits of opponents.
- Q Pay attention to the play of trumps by opponents.
- Q Create entries by ruffing winners.
- Q Adopt a forcing defence with good trumps and a good side suit.
- Q Develop advanced attitude signals.
- Q Pay attention to penalty doubles.

Ruffing and forcing are effective techniques to produce defensive winners. Hands in this chapter remind defenders to time their ruffs and their forcing defence. In one, you sit safely with KJ three-card behind AQ10, but the only defence is to give partner a ruff. Two world champions missed the defence. There is a hand where Q10 three-trump was worse than three-small, allowing declarer to land a shadowy contract. Cooperative defence relies on accurate signaling. The chapter ends with hands where world champions failed to recognise each other's intriguing signals. As usual, the focus is on the queens.

The detective

2007 USA	♠ A10853		
Betty Kaplan teams	♡ 76		
W/ Both vulnerable	◇ QJ104		
	♣ 86		

♠ KQ		♠ J962
♡ 1085		♡ KQJ
◇ A875		◇ K962
♣ J1054		♣ 93

♠ 74
♡ A9432
◇ 3
♣ AKQ72

West	North	East	South
Hand		Greenberg	Fout
Pass	Pass	Pass	1♡
Pass	1♠	Pass	2♣
Pass	2♡		

Detecting a concealed singleton can be fun. Hand sat West and led the king of spades against 2♡. Declarer won with dummy's ace and ducked a heart to the jack. East returned a spade to the queen. West studied the clues surrounding the queens.

The first hint was a duck of the jack of hearts. It implied a queen and good trump holding of partner, and possibly two tricks. The second hint was the idling of the club suit bid by declarer. There were no impending ruffs or establishment, reflecting solid clubs. Hand deduced that declarer had a 2-5-1-5 shape. This led to the third hint based on the weakness shown in the bidding. The diamond singleton would not be the king.

Hand underled his diamond. East won his king. An impeccable jack of spades followed. Hand scored a trump trick, overruffing the nine with his ten. East had one more trump trick. The detective's fourth club set the impregnable contract.

Jackstraw

2006 Rosenblum Cup
N/ EW vulnerable

```
                    ♠ 986532
                    ♡ A7
                    ◊ J632
                    ♣ K
      ♠ AQ74                      ♠ KJ10
      ♡ 982                       ♡ KJ653
      ◊ A5                        ◊ Q4
      ♣ 9864                      ♣ AQ7
                    ♠ —
                    ♡ Q104
                    ◊ K10987
                    ♣ J10532
```

West	North	East	South
McIntosh	Upmath	Bakhshi	Torngvist
	Pass	1NT	2NT
Double	4◊	4♡	Pass
Pass	Double		

It is a joy to set a doubled contract with ruffs. South hit upon a splendid club lead, his partner's singleton, in 4♡ doubled. He chose the ten to signal a void in spades, to the king and declarer's ace. Surveying the scene, Bakhshi advanced the jack of hearts. South could not resist taking with his queen, and returned a club for a likely ruff. Fortunately, North trumped, but unfortunately it was the ace. South compounded the misfortune when he ruffed the compliant return of a spade, at the expense of his natural trump trick. That was the third and last trick for the defence.

Jackstraws is a game in which players gently withdraw straws, one by one, from a pile. Remove the wrong straw and the pile collapses. To change destiny, South should have resisted touching the fatal jackstraw. Based on the play and the penalty double, partner should have a trump higher than the jack. After taking the jack, North would give South a ruff in spades. South would return a club for North to ruff. A further spade would allow South to ruff with his queen. Three crossruffs and the ace of hearts would sink the contract. Ironically, if South's three hearts were mini, he would defeat the hand effortlessly.

An unnecessary surplus

2001 Bermuda Bowl
USA1 v Italy
S/ EW vulnerable

```
                    ♠ A9832
                    ♡ A
                    ◇ 1064
                    ♣ AQ97
   ♠ K54                              ♠ 1076
   ♡ Q10987                           ♡ K6532
   ◇ KJ3                              ◇ 9
   ♣ K5                               ♣ J862
                    ♠ QJ
                    ♡ J4
                    ◇ AQ8752
                    ♣ 1043
```

West	North	East	South
Duboin	Hamman	Bocchi	Soloway
			Pass
1♡	1♠	3◇ (weak♡ raise)	Pass
Pass	Double	Pass	4♠

Meckstroth	Versace	Rodwell	Lauria
			Pass
1♡	1♠	3◇ (weak♡ raise)	Double
3♡	Double	Pass	3♠
Pass	4◇	Pass	4♠

We decline to ruff our winners. This deal featured a clash of the giants. Italy eliminated USA1 but lost to Norway. Norway squandered a 79-IMP lead at the half and succumbed to USA2 in the final.

Each East led his diamond, a sonorous singleton. Each declarer played low in dummy. Meckstroth and Duboin, as West, won with the jack and returned a heart to the ace. Declarers led a spade to dummy's jack. USA's West won with his king and returned a club. Declarer finessed his queen. Italy's West also won with his king. He returned his king of clubs to the ace. After leading a spade to the queen in dummy, declarers ruffed a heart, drew the remaining trumps with the ace, and led a diamond to the queen and king. The good diamonds in dummy dispatched the losing clubs. Declarers lost two diamonds and a spade for ten tricks and 420.

Based on the lead and the bidding, declarer was likely to be 5-1-3-4. Competing to 3♡ at unfavourable vulnerability, and not having AK of hearts, East should have reasonable clubs. Declarer needed the diamonds for tricks. The only entry in dummy was the shaky spades after exhausting declarer's diamonds. A diamond attack was not fanciful or foolish. After taking the opening lead, West returned a diamond. East ruffed. Declarer took the return of a heart or a club. He could not play a spade to the jack. West's last diamond gave East a ruff, setting the contract. If declarer played the ace and queen of spades smothering East's ten, West would take his king and sail a diamond. Dummy could not enjoy the diamonds, as West had a trump. Declarers conceded a club, for down one.

Both Wests missed a charismatic defence. The knee-jerk reaction—that the king of diamonds should await the queen—was illusory. Rather, the king of spades was a key card guarding the queen. The humour was that declarers might make the same play with the jack of diamonds. With king third, West would fly a diamond at the second trick. The jack was an unnecessary surplus.

Flying over a Great Wall

		♠ K743	
1997 USA		♡ 93	
Grand National teams		◇ KQ109	
W/ Both vulnerable		♣ A32	

♠ AQ10			♠ 62
♡ AJ4			♡ KQ1065
◇ A8754			◇ J63
♣ K6			♣ Q97

		♠ J985	
		♡ 872	
		◇ 2	
		♣ J10854	

West	*North*	*East*	*South*
Martel	Rotman	Stansby	Peres
1◇	Pass	1♡	Pass
2NT	Pass	3♣	Pass
3♡	Pass	3NT	Pass
4♡			

We sometimes need unnecessary ruffs to create entries. South led his diamond. Identifying it as a singleton, declarer played dummy's ace. He led the king of clubs to the ace. North cashed the queen of diamonds. Peres sat South. He ruffed his partner's winner.

Peres foresaw that his partner would cash the king of diamonds, and led a fourth diamond, hoping for a promotion in trumps. Due to his weak trumps, Peres knew this defence would falter. Rather, dummy's fifth diamond provided a discard for declarer. North needed a relevant king for the setting trick behind the strong dummy.

If the king were in spades, South could not wait until the third diamond. When South ruffed the third diamond and returned a spade, declarer won with dummy's ace, cashed the queen of clubs, ruffed a club in dummy, ruffed a diamond, drew trumps, and enjoyed the fifth diamond for ten tricks. Declarer seemed to be protected by dummy's Great Wall. To fly over it, Peres ruffed the second diamond and flew back a spade. The third diamond was an entry for North to enjoy the king of spades for down one.

An illusory cross-ruff

2004 Olympiad	♠ AQ
France v Brazil	♡ QJ5
N/ EW vulnerable	◊ AJ
	♣ J86542

♠ 854		♠ KJ9
♡ A10643		♡ 9
◊ K872		◊ Q10963
♣ 7		♣ AQ93

	♠ 107632
	♡ K872
	◊ 54
	♣ K10

West	North	East	South
Villas Boas	Multon	Chagas	Quantin
	1NT (strong)	Pass	2♡
Double	Pass	Pass	2♠

Defenders need to time their ruffs. Sitting East was Chagas, who has won two world champion teams for Brazil. He took West's lead of a club, clearly a singleton, with his ace. An unimpeachable return of hearts, the suit doubled by partner, should yield a few cross-ruffs. The usually fluid Chagas, holding two valuable queens, paused. Partner should lead a heart if he had the ace and king. Declarer possessed ♡K and ♣K. As he showed weakness in the bidding, he should have only five spades and no more high cards.

East's trumps were bound for two tricks, the ingredients for a forcing defence. Ruffs could wait, as club ruffs now could set up the suit for declarer. Chagas led back not a club, nor a heart, but a delicate diamond to the king and ace. Quantin, a world team champion, expertly played the ace and queen of spades. East took with his king and led a club. West ruffed and returned a diamond to the queen. East forced declarer with a third diamond. Declarer ruffed and played hearts, forcing out the ace. West played the fourth diamond. Declarer ruffed. His remaining trump and heart were losers. He conceded down two, minus 100.

South played the same contract in the other room. East took the lead with the ace of clubs and led a heart to West's ace. East ruffed a heart. West ruffed a club. East ruffed the third heart, and could have returned a diamond to beat the contract. Immersed in the joy of ruffing, East instead tried another club. Declarer ruffed with the ten. When West failed to overruff, declarer played a spade to the ace, dropping the king. The queen drew West's remaining trump. Declarer ruffed a club in hand. The ace of diamonds was the entry to enjoy the clubs for 110. It was embarrassing for the defenders to halt after taking the first five tricks. Chagas boasted seven.

A law of physics

2005 Wales
W/ Both vulnerable

	♠ 753	
	♡ AJ2	
	◊ 8643	
	♣ QJ8	

♠ Q94		♠ K2
♡ KQ763		♡ 10954
◊ KQJ		◊ A10975
♣ 65		♣ A3

	♠ AJ1086	
	♡ 8	
	◊ 2	
	♣ K109742	

West	North	East	South
John	Ratcliff	Charlesworth	Jourdain
1♡	Pass	2◊	2NT
3◊	3♡	4♡	4♠

A forcing defence requires cooperation. North-South did well reaching 4♠, with a cue bid of 3♡ from North. West led ◊KQ. Declarer ruffed the second diamond. If he were to use the ace of hearts as an entry for the finesse in trumps, he would expose himself to forces in hearts from East. Jourdain intelligently played a club to the jack and ace. Declarer ruffed the return of a third diamond, played a club to the queen, and led a spade to the ten and queen. West had no diamonds to force declarer. The ace of heart provided an entry to finesse again in spades, scoring 620.

Declarer announced his two suits by bidding 2NT. The early club to dummy's jack, risking a ruff, aroused curiosity. When holding an ace in declarer's suit, it is usually clever to duck. If East allowed the jack of clubs to stand, declarer would use this premature entry to finesse a spade to the queen. West attacked with his third diamond. Declarer ruffed and had two trumps left. If he crossed to the ace of hearts for a finesse in trumps, or dropped the trump king, he could not draw the remaining trump without establishing the clubs. If he led a club to the queen and ace, East would force with the fourth diamond. Declarer could not ruff without giving a trump trick to the defence, and went down.

Based on count signals on the first club, East should detect declarer's 5-1-1-6 shape. West bid twice. A trump honour with West was a legitimate expectation. A forcing defence was writing on the wall. West held three diamonds. East should therefore let partner force declarer with a third diamond and preserve his ace of clubs for a fourth diamond. It was a law of physics: two forces are mightier than one. The law is instructive to defenders with shorter forcing suits: act promptly with your entries.

Beauty with a mask

		♠ A932	
2001 European Cup (women)		♡ 2	
Germany v Israel		◊ A86	
S/ Both vulnerable		♣ AQ654	

	♠ QJ876		♠ —
	♡ 9754		♡ AKQ63
	◊ J7		◊ K9532
	♣ J2		♣ 1073

		♠ K1054	
		♡ J108	
		◊ Q104	
		♣ K98	

West	North	East	South
West	*North*	*East*	*South*
Levit-Porat	Auken	Campanile	von Armin
			Pass
Pass	1♠	2♡	2♠
Pass	Pass	Double	Redouble
3♡	Double		

This hand shows forcing defence in a new dimension. The German pair showed their calibre in 1989 when they reached the semifinal of the Venice Cup. They won the Cup in 1995 and 2001 and enjoyed worldwide recognition.

West judged well not to defend 2♠ doubled. South was looking for heavy penalties when she defended 3♡ doubled. She led a spade to dummy's jack and ace. Declarer ruffed and led a club to the queen. North returned a trump, taken by declarer. She played a second club. South took with her king and returned a second trump. Declarer took the trick, ruffed a club in dummy, led a diamond to her king, and played another diamond. South won with the queen and played a third trump. Declarer sailed a third diamond. When the ten and ace clashed, her diamonds were good, making 730.

The defenders forced declarer with the lead. They switched industriously, exhausting dummy's trumps. The defence needed to force declarer twice. North could overtake the queen with her ace of diamonds and return a spade. If declarer ruffed the spade, declarer, South, and West would have one trump each. As the diamonds were not established, she could ruff a diamond in dummy. She had to ruff a spade back, but that was her remaining trump, and South still had a trump going down aplenty. A better choice was ducking the coercive second spade. South took with her king and played a third trump. The ten of diamonds set the contract for minus 200.

An overtaking of the queen of diamonds required knowledge of the ten. South should therefore Queen Duck on the second diamond. North should discover the complete layout to return a spade. There were two defensive tasks: drawing dummy's trumps and forcing declarer as she might have long diamonds. Accurate defence count signals on the minors should help. Declarer's cute double in the second round masked her beautifully shaped hand and was preparatory for a penalty-pass if West held strong spades.

Mr. and Mrs. Smith

		♠ 8	
2006 McConnell Cup semifinal		♡ AJ974	
USA/ Russia v China		◊ KJ94	
W/ NS vulnerable		♣ QJ7	

♠ AJ1076		♠ KQ953
♡ KQ3		♡ 8
◊ 75		◊ AQ86
♣ 985		♣ K63

	♠ 42	
	♡ 10652	
	◊ 1032	
	♣ A1042	

West	North	East	South
L P Wang	Sokolow	Yu Zhang	Molson
1♠	Double	2♡ (forcing)	Pass
2♠	Pass	4♡ (♠ fit)	Pass
4♠			

Ponomareva	W F Wang	Gromova	H L Wang
Pass	1♡	1♠	2♡
2NT	3◊	4♠	

This hand is not about ruffs. It emphasizes the difficulty in defence signals. China led by 25 IMPs going into the last session. In the first room, China's West declared 4♠ after her Precision opening of 1♠. She received a trump lead. After two rounds of trumps, declarer led a heart to the king and ace. Seeing dummy's king, North returned the queen of clubs for down one, plus 50.

In the other room, natural biddings arrived at the same contract declared by East. North's 3◊ re-bid was instrumental. South led the two of diamonds, promising a ten or an honour. The king lost to declarer's ace. After drawing trumps, declarer again led a heart to the king and ace. Not knowing East's hand, North elected to return a diamond. Declarer won with the queen, ruffed a diamond in dummy, and pitched a club on the queen of hearts. She lost two clubs, making 420, and won by 3 IMPs. Her team won the final.

As declarer held four diamonds, a winner in diamonds could wait. South should hold an honour in clubs. The Chinese pairs were not regular partnerships. Adopting Smith signal, South played the ten on the first heart, expressing lack of interest in diamonds. Buoyed with confidence, North would shift to her queen of clubs to win the match. China was compensated when they won the McConnell Cup in 2010.

An old vintage

1999 USA Fall National	♠ 432	
Open pairs	♡ Q62	
N/ Neither vulnerable	◇ 53	
	♣ KQ1073	

	♠ KQ10		♠ A8765
	♡ 1073		♡ 9854
	◇ K1062		◇ J7
	♣ AJ2		♣ 98

	♠ J9	
	♡ AKJ	
	◇ AQ984	
	♣ 654	

West	North	East	South
Robinson	van Prooijen	Boyd	de Wijs
	Pass	Pass	1NT
Pass	3NT		

We continue with intriguing defence signals. Declarer was de Wijs. He opened 1NT with two suits unguarded. West chose his longest suit and led the deuce of diamonds. Declarer knew his spades would soon be slaughtered if he did not do something extraordinary. He smoothly accepted East's jack with his sublime ace, not the queen of diamonds. A club to his king held. de Wijs returned to hand with the ace of hearts and played another club, ducked by West. Declarer continued with a third club to the ace. West philosophised for an exit card.

East followed clubs in reverse order, a Smith pinpointing weakness in diamonds, or showing count. Partner played the four on the ace of hearts and discarded the nine of hearts on the third club. While the signals in clubs might show count, the nine of hearts reiterated lack of interest in diamonds. East-West had enjoyed a long partnership, winning the Rosenblum Cup in 1986. It was not enough, however, to overcome the facts at the first trick. West cashed the king of diamonds and returned a diamond, eagerly anticipating a Queen Discovery from East. de Wijs took eleven tricks instead of seven. His camouflage was an old vintage. For once, one hidden queen defeated four defence signals.

5

CREATIVE ENTRIES

TIPS FOR
Entries and Communication

Q   Organise a ruffing plan.

Q   Sacrifice your queen or jack to avoid an endplay.

Q   Chase your 3NT tricks before the opponents.

Q   Develop a suit only if there are entries.

Q   Examine entries to attack communication of opponents.

Q   Explore creative entries in weak hands by unconventional ducks.

Q   Induce opponents to release premature winners.

Entries and communication often decide the fate of contracts. This chapter describes the chasing of tricks competed over by declarers and defenders. A defender massages a dummy, forcing it to release winners prematurely, thereby losing tricks in that suit and, ultimately, the contract. Another defender jettisons all four of his jacks, creating an entry for partner to defeat a contract. In "Archimedes' principle," a defender refuses to lift up declarer's ninth trick in 3NT, although it sets up his partner's suit. Queens remain our focus, with hands also involving enterprising jacks, companions of queens.

A rising jack

2007 Bermuda Bowl
Poland v Italy
E/ Both vulnerable

	♠ Q86	
	♡ AQJ	
	◇ KQ54	
	♣ A94	

♠ A43		♠ 105
♡ K953		♡ 64
◇ AJ8		◇ 10973
♣ 732		♣ KQJ108

	♠ KJ972	
	♡ 10872	
	◇ 62	
	♣ 65	

West	*North*	*East*	*South*
Nunes	Gawrys	Fantoni	Chmurski
		Pass	Pass
1NT	Double	Redouble	Pass
2♣	Pass	Pass	2♠
Pass	3♣	Pass	3♡
Pass	4♠		
Jassem	Bocchi	Martens	Duboin
		Pass	Pass
1♣	Double	Pass	1♡ (♠)
Pass	1NT	2♣	2♡ (transfer)
Pass	2♠		

This hand is about unblocking. 1NT in the second room was a "marionette," a non-acceptance showing fewer than four spades. The fashionable transfer failed to reach the popular 4♠. In the first room, Poland reached it naturally. West led the deuce of clubs, ducked to the jack. East returned a club to dummy's ace. A trump was played to the king and ace. West returned a spade to the jack. Declarer led a heart to dummy's jack, cashed the queen of spades, and ruffed a club in hand. He finessed a second heart to the queen, and thought it proper to cash the ace of hearts. The operation failed, as he had a loser in hearts and in diamonds: down one and minus 100.

There was a winning strategy. After declarer drew trumps and ruffed the third club, he advanced a diamond. West not only must duck; he also needed to rise with the jack, a Bath coup variation. Otherwise, after the queen of diamonds and a small diamond, West would be endplayed with his jack. If he cashed the ace of diamonds, declarer would ruff and finesse a heart to the queen. The king of diamonds would dispatch the fourth heart in hand, making 620. If West returned a heart after scoring his treasured jack, declarer would finesse the queen and ruff a diamond in hand, dropping the ace. The ace of hearts in dummy was the entry to enjoy the king of diamonds. The rising jack allowed East take the second diamond with his ten and play clubs. Declarer could ruff but would have to lose to the diamond ace.

Rodwell of USA showed a witty strategy. He led a diamond towards dummy after the second spade, making it difficult for West, Bertheau of Sweden, to "jack." Bertheau rose with his ace, solving declarer's problems. Declarer had three entries in trumps. He required four entries to the diamonds and hearts. He could create another entry by playing the jack of spades on the first spade, the queen on the second spade, and overtaking with his king on seeing the ten from East. No declarer appeared to have made that far-sighted play.

A tale of four jacks

2009 Sweden
E/ Neither vulnerable

		♠ A105	
		♡ A9654	
		◇ 86	
		♣ 543	

♠ 842
♡ Q7
◇ 10742
♣ 10972

♠ QJ63
♡ J103
◇ AJ3
♣ AJ6

♠ K97
♡ K82
◇ KQ95
♣ KQ8

West	North	East	South
		Fredin	
		1♠	1NT
Pass	2◇ (transfer)	Pass	2♡
Pass	2NT	Pass	3NT

Fredin, as East, was loaded with four jacks. He played his first jack when West led a spade. Declarer played his king, crossed to the ace of hearts in dummy, and led a diamond. East played his second jack, a Jack Sacrifice, to the queen. Declarer played the king of hearts and a heart, endplaying East.

Consistent with his play, Fredin played his fourth jack, the club. His second Jack Sacrifice continued the strategy of creating entries to West. After chewing another jack with the queen of clubs, declarer attempted a diamond. West produced the magical ten, a reward for the four jack-jettisons. The lead of a spade through dummy yielded a fifth defensive trick. Holding a strong hand against 3NT, Fredin overcame an adverse Bath coup by two impressive and inspirational Jack Sacrifices.

Achilles' heel

		♠ K96	
2004 Olympiad quarterfinal		♡ A86	
Italy v Pakistan		◇ AQ10	
S/ EW vulnerable		♣ AQ74	

♠ AQ1084			♠ J5
♡ Q743			♡ 1092
◇ 983			◇ KJ62
♣ 5			♣ 9832

		♠ 732	
		♡ KJ5	
		◇ 754	
		♣ KJ106	

West	North	East	South
Versace	Hadi	Lauria	Shoaib
			Pass
Pass	1♣	Pass	2♣
Double	Redouble	Pass	Pass
2♠	2NT	Pass	3NT

Fazli	Bocchi	Allana	Duboin
			Pass
Pass	2♣	Pass	2♠
Double	2NT	Pass	3NT

Defenders relied on entries to defeat 3NT. Both Easts led the jack of spades, the suit bid by partner. In the second room, West ducked and took the second spade. He continued spades to the king. Bocchi crossed to dummy with the ten of clubs and finessed a diamond to his ten and jack. East, having no spades, led the ten of hearts, covered by the jack, queen, and ace. Declarer cleared clubs, played the king of hearts, and a heart to the nine. East was endplayed, having to lead diamonds into declarer's AQ for minus 400. East exposed his ten and nine of hearts; otherwise, declarer would need to read double dummy, playing an anti-percentage jack of hearts through West for the throw-in. A pedestrian second finesse in diamonds, followed by finesse in hearts, would doom the contract.

In the other room, Versace, as West, overtook the opening lead with his queen and switched to diamonds. East took the queen with his king and returned a spade. Versace won his ace and attacked a second diamond to the ten and jack. East returned a diamond. The remaining hope for declarer was the heart finesse. It lost and Italy scored a game swing. They successfully defended their Olympiad title. Knowing his lack of entries, Versace discovered greener pastures. A weak suit in dummy is often an Achilles' heel.

Give dummy a massage

2005 USA Fall National	♠ J7	
Open pairs	♡ Q9643	
W/ Both vulnerable	◊ 9	
	♣ AKQ102	

	♠ KQ2		♠ A843
	♡ AJ75		♡ 108
	◊ 1087		◊ J642
	♣ 854		♣ J63

	♠ 10965	
	♡ K2	
	◊ AKQ53	
	♣ 97	

West	North	East	South
Versace		Jacobs	
Pass	1♡	Pass	2◊
Pass	3♣	Pass	3◊
Pass	3NT		

3NT is a chase of tricks contested between declarers and defenders. Sometimes a queen directs you to the winning path. East led the three of spades to the queen, an indication that declarer did not hold the ace of spades. If East possessed the jack defence had five tricks. Versace gauged that declarer was likely to be 2-5-1-5. Even if he held the diamond jack, he could not overtake in dummy to run the diamonds. Three diamonds, five solid clubs, and a possible queen of hearts added up to nine tricks.

If declarer had a 2-5-2-4 shape, the defence needed to cash tricks quickly. Versace assessed this alternative in conjunction with East holding the jack of spades and decided against continuing spades. His ace of hearts guarded against the king as an entry to dummy. A fifth defensive trick in the minors was possible. He tested the waters with a lovely diamond. Declarer knew his fate. Hoping for a minor miracle, he cashed three diamonds prematurely and led a heart towards his queen. Versace greeted with his ace, cashed his king of spades, and returned a spade to the ace. East cashed the fourth diamond, sinking the contract. Versace massaged the dummy to release a vital defensive trick.

Basic instinct

2009 Yeh Brothers Cup final	♠ 1098		
Netherlands v Sweden	♡ Q75		
E/ Neither vulnerable	◇ AJ85		
	♣ 1098		
	♠ KQ		♠ J6543
	♡ A962		♡ 1083
	◇ 74		◇ 32
	♣ KJ743		♣ Q62
	♠ A72		
	♡ KJ4		
	◇ KQ1096		
	♣ A5		

West	*North*	*East*	*South*
Bertheau	Drijver	Nystrom	Brink
		Pass	1♣ (artificial)
Pass	1NT	Pass	3NT
Bakkeren	Fredin	Bertens	Fallenius
		Pass	1♣ (artificial)
Pass	1NT	Pass	2◇
Pass	3NT		

This hand demonstrates a skillful play or defence surrounding the queens. In both rooms, the lead was the three of spades, third or fifth best. When Fredin was declarer, he thought it was from the fifth and ducked in dummy. It was basic instinct. Bakkeren won his queen. Knowing that partner should not have more than a side queen, there was no future in spades. He switched to clubs, his strong suit. East was a faithful partner, producing a relevant queen. The ace of hearts was the entry to run the clubs for down two and 100.

Drijver evaluated the lead. West must have an honour. If it was a doubleton with the king, he might accidentally play small on dummy's ace. If it was ♠KQ, there was no worry. If it was ♠KJ or ♠QJ doubleton, his ♠1098 were good stoppers. Spades could break 4-3. A duck of the first spade would benefit only if East held the ace of hearts and West held a doubleton spade with one honour. If West held the ace of hearts, a shift to clubs seemed imminent. It was not clear if mathematical probability or basic instinct swung the decision. Drijver rose with dummy's ace and played hearts to force out the ace, scoring 400. Netherlands won and collected US$76,000.

Archimedes' principle

1997 UK
London TGR
S/ Neither vulnerable

	♠ J873		
	♡ A2		
	◇ KQJ5		
	♣ J64		
♠ A65		♠ K1092	
♡ 6543		♡ K87	
◇ 32		◇ 10987	
♣ K1082		♣ Q5	
	♠ Q4		
	♡ QJ109		
	◇ A64		
	♣ A973		

West	North	East	South
		Hallberg	
			1NT (13-15)
Pass	2♣	Pass	2♡
Pass	3NT		

Archimedes explained the physics of buoyancy, describing the forces that make an object float—or not. I describe the following defence as a "sinking return." In 3NT, West led a club to the queen and ace. Declarer played the ace of hearts, led a heart to his queen, and continued hearts with the jack to the king, discarding a spade in dummy. Most at East automatically returned a club, lifting the jack in dummy. Declarer had nine tricks.

Hallberg diagnosed that declarer should have the queen of spades and the ace of diamonds. The return of a club would float up a ninth trick for declarer. He sailed a diamond. If declarer took with his ace, he would have to cash the fourth heart and dummy had no suitable discard. If he did not cash the heart and led a club, he would have no entry to score the fourth heart. In summary, declarer required two further entries in hand to float a club up and to cash his heart. The sailing of a diamond sunk the winning ninth trick.

Switching your front line

		♠ 74	
2002 European Cup		♡ J104	
Italy v Bulgaria		◊ Q87	
W/ EW vulnerable		♣ A10986	

♠ AKQ2		♠ 93
♡ 96		♡ KQ82
◊ K52		◊ A10943
♣ J743		♣ K2

	♠ J10865	
	♡ A753	
	◊ J6	
	♣ Q5	

West	*North*	*East*	*South*
Nanev	Sementa	Minov	Versace
1◊	Pass	1♡	1♠
Pass	Pass	2♠	Pass
3NT			

Duboin	Stamatov	Bocchi	Karaivanov
1♣	Pass	1◊	Pass
1NT	Pass	3NT	

Both rooms declared 3NT. In the second room, North led the ten of clubs. Dummy played small. South took with the queen and returned a club to the ace. North continued clubs. Declarer won with his jack and led a diamond to the ten and jack. South had no more clubs to return. Declarer later forced out the ace of hearts, scoring three spades, one heart, four diamonds, and a club for 600. A tactical duck by South on the first trick could be countered elegantly by declarer by following small in hand.

In the first room, Versace, as South, took the lead with his queen of clubs. He deduced that partner held the ace but was unlikely to have an entry to enjoy clubs. He switched to the jack of spades, to the ace. Declarer led a diamond to the nine and jack. Versace persisted with his plan of disrupting communication. He attacked a second spade with the ten, to declarer's king. Declarer played a club. North took his ace and returned a diamond to the king. Declarer had already lost three tricks. As he had not knocked out the ace of hearts, he refrained from cashing his winner in spades or clubs. Instead, he attempted a pressure play by cashing the diamonds. In the ending, dummy had ♡KQ82, losing two tricks for down one. If he had cashed the jack of clubs, dummy had ♡KQ8, again losing two tricks at the end.

If declarer does not cash the diamonds and tries the nine of hearts, covered by the ten and ducked in dummy, North returns a diamond. If dummy covers the ten of hearts, South ducks. There might be other playing paths. The result should still be down one. If declarer does not play to the king of clubs after taking the second spade, and leads the heart nine to North's ten and dummy's queen, South ducks. Declarer returns to his king of diamonds and lead a heart, North puts up the jack to force dummy's king. Whether or not South ducks, his ♡75 limits dummy's ♡82 to one trick. As the queen of spades was in the wilderness, declarer had only eight tricks.

To understand the switch by Versace after his queen of clubs, recall Bakkeren's successful switch after realizing that his partner would not have a side entry. For similar reasons, Hallberg refrained from establishing the long suit of his partner, thereby denying declarer a vital trick. Versace performed a combination here.

A vanishing king

2005 Senior Bowl
Italy v Japan
N/ NS vulnerable

	♠ AK72	
	♡ AQ	
	◇ 97654	
	♣ J7	

♠ Q6		♠ 1098
♡ 865		♡ J9732
◇ 102		◇ AJ3
♣ A109854		♣ K2

	♠ J543	
	♡ K104	
	◇ KQ8	
	♣ Q63	

West	*North*	*East*	*South*
Forquet	Abe	Masucci	Ino
	1◇	Pass	2NT
Pass	3NT		

The significance of entries was the major consideration in this hand. South showed a balanced hand by bidding 2NT instead of 1♠. The lead of a diamond to the ace, followed by the king of clubs and a club, would promote a trick in trumps for the defence to defeat 4♠.

In 3NT, West led the ten of clubs. If East stepped up with his king and continued clubs, West would duck to the jack. Declarer would drop the queen of spades in two rounds and force out the ace of diamonds. East would have no clubs to return, and declarer would score ten tricks for 630.

Unless his partner held an unlikely honour in diamonds, East could anticipate four diamond tricks for declarer when declarer led diamonds through his vulnerable ◇AJ3. There were at least four tricks in the majors. A ninth was available from a relevant king or queen in the majors, or the ♣A. The ♣10 appeared to be from a long suit headed by a sole honour. Banking on West having the ♣A as his best hope, Masucci, as East, ducked the ♣10 lead at this table. We learned earlier that declarer could counter elegantly by ducking, which was extremely clever if East held ♣Kx but shamefully naive if defenders next cashed an avalanche of clubs. Opting for injury over insult, declarer mechanically took the ♣10 with his ♣Q. When a diamond from dummy was greeted by East with his ace, a return of the vanishing ♣K for West to cover produced five winners for down two. Predictably, all other nineteen 3NT declarers made their contracts.

6

QUEEN DEFENCE

TIPS FOR
Queen Defence

- Q Organise a ruffing plan.
- Q Identify Doomed Queens.
- Q Drop a Doomed Queen as early as possible.
- Q Perform the Queen Drop smoothly.
- Q Drop the ten or nine to hide a Doomed Queen in partner.
- Q Display high cards to hide a crucial queen.
- Q Divert declarer away from playing a suit with a Doomed Queen.

This chapter introduces hands featuring Queen (King) Hiding, Queen Seeking, and the Queen Drop—techniques to divert declarer from a winning line. There are hands where defenders hid their queens, dropped their queens as camouflage, or extracted a safe queen from opponents. The last hand features a Queen Sacrifice working against the same world champion for a second time. Readers may feel encouraged that the spectacular plays were often performed by less well known players against renowned experts.

Queen defence

Defend
skillfully with
the queens.

Queen defence

Queen hiding

Hide a
crucial queen.

Queen hiding

Queen seeking

Play a queen
unnecessarily
or
unnaturally.

Queen seeking

doomed **Q**ueen

A queen that
can be
naturally
finessed or
dropped.

doomed **Q**ueen

Queen drop

Discard a
queen
unnecessarily,
knowing it is
doomed.

Queen drop

Hiding partner's queen

2007 Bermuda Bowl
Sweden v Brazil
N/ Both vulnerable

```
                    ♠ 92
                    ♡ Q64
                    ◊ Q98
                    ♣ J7653
        ♠ K43                       ♠ QJ108765
        ♡ KJ983                     ♡ A75
        ◊ 743                       ◊ A2
        ♣ A4                        ♣ 10
                    ♠ A
                    ♡ 102
                    ◊ KJ1065
                    ♣ KQ982
```

West	North	East	South
Figueiredo	Efraimsson	Brenner	Morath
	Pass	1♠	2NT
3◊ (♠ support)	5♣	5♠	

Bertheau	Chagas	Nystrom	Villas Boas
	Pass	1♠	2NT
3◊ (♠ support)	5♣	5◊	Pass
5♠			

The hands in this chapter are related to my 1993 Bols Tip of queening your defence. For this first hand, most North-South succeeded pushing opponents to 5♠. In the first room, Brenner, as declarer, took the lead with the ace of clubs in dummy and drew trumps. South was Morath. Taking his ace, and noting the play of the discouraging jack of clubs by North on the first club, South returned crucially a diamond to the queen and ace. Declarer had to locate the queen of hearts to make his contract. He drew the remaining trump and played the king of hearts.

The bidding marked North with more hearts and the favourite to hold the queen. Declarer intended to play the jack of hearts, pinning a 10x in South. Morath was alert and dropped the ten under the king. Declarer gauged Morath to have Q10 doubleton. His next play of a small heart to the ace doomed the contract for minus 100.

In the other room, South led an imaginative diamond. After losing the ace of trumps and a diamond, declarer led a heart towards dummy. It was more difficult for South to put up the ten. Nystrom drew the same inference, put up the king, and advanced the jack of hearts to score 650. The Queening play by Morath successfully hid partner's queen. The victory points gained in this hand lifted Sweden and South Africa to quarterfinal spots, edging out Brazil. Norway defeated USA1 in the final.

Hiding a king

2001 USA
Blue Ribbon pairs
N/ NS vulnerable

	♠ 104	
	♡ 8765	
	◇ 1062	
	♣ K752	

♠ 532		♠ AKQJ76
♡ J432		♡ AQ109
◇ 93		◇ QJ
♣ AJ43		♣ 9

♠ 98
♡ K
◇ AK8754
♣ Q1086

West	North	East	South
			1◇
Pass	Pass	Double	Pass
1♡	Pass	4♠	

Hiding kings is next. Ralph Cohen sat East. 4♡ was fraught with danger, losing two top diamonds and being forced with a club shift. Declarer had to handle the offside king of hearts and the 4-1 break in trumps. Abandoning the fit in hearts, Cohen settled for his six-card solid suit and declared 4♠. After cashing his ◇AK, South shifted to a trump. Declarer drew trumps, played a club to the ace, and led the jack of hearts. Putting up the ace, he had 11 tricks, scoring 55 of 64 match points.

South held a Doomed Queen in clubs if declarer had the king—unlikely, judging from the play. Unless partner had a singleton or doubleton club with the king, going up with the queen on the first club posed little risk. A pretension of holding KQ of clubs, the high-card points required for an opening bid, denied the king of hearts by implication. The lack of interest from South on the first club alerted declarer, who dropped the singleton king. The Queen Seeking play of the queen of clubs was a Bols Tip recommendation. South missed an opportunity to hide his singleton status.

A revealing singleton

2001 Venice Cup final	♠ 84		
Germany v France	♡ K86		
W/ Both vulnerable	◇ 7632		
	♣ A632		

♠ QJ953		♠ K76
♡ Q43		♡ 105
◇ KJ109		◇ Q54
♣ 4		♣ KQ1087

♠ A102
♡ AJ972
◇ A8
♣ J95

West	North	East	South
Bessis	*Auken*	*d'Ovidio*	*von Armin*
Pass	Pass	Pass	1♡
1♠	Double	2♠	Double
Pass	2NT (ask)	Pass	3♡

This hand features three Bols Tips. It decided the 2001 Venice Cup in France. The original venue of picturesque Bali was deemed unsafe after 9/11. France did not secure a European berth for its women's team. But they qualified as host and led by 45.5 IMPs going into the last session. However, a string of enterprising swings from Auken and von Armin kept them from victory.

Von Armin faced many queen-finding missions in this final session. She had missed a vital queen on her left, whose system prevented an opening of 1NT with eighteen points. She had dropped a doubleton queen in another hand, missing four-card. Towards the end, a weak-two opening on her left left a key jack semi-exposed on her right. She finessed successfully. The diagrammed hand tested her Queen Discovery skill again.

In the other room, France, with a ruff in diamonds, defeated 2♠ for 100. In this room, Germany competed to 3♥. West led her club. Declarer identified its singleton nature. She rose reasonably with dummy's ace. On reflection, it worked better playing small. West should have longer trumps. Her ruff of a club might be at the expense of a winner. The risk was a second ruff if East had another entry, but East needed to possess two honours in spades or in diamonds.

A computer calculation would give the advantage to ducking the lead. Meanwhile, von Armin focused on keeping East off the lead and inserted her ten when she led a spade from dummy. West played her jack and led an intellectual but standard jack of diamonds. East and declarer played small. Declarer took the continuation of a diamond with her ace. She deduced from the lead and the bidding that spades broke 5-3 and hearts broke 3-2, with length in West. West might have ♠KJ or ♠QJ. Her diamonds should include ◊KJ. More importantly, West should be 5-3-4-1.

West should therefore hold the queen of hearts for her overcall, and East likely did not hold it or else would have opened. The backward finesse required a doubleton ten of hearts with East. Von Armin ventured her jack of hearts hopefully through West. It held. She cashed the ace of spades and ruffed a spade in dummy. She cashed the king of hearts, ruffed a diamond in hand, and played the ace of hearts, drawing the queen for 140, plus 1 IMP. A normal play in trumps would be down one, minus 5 IMPs. The margin of victory was 3.5 IMPs. Germany would also win the match defending 2♠.

West did not compete to 3♠. The results in both rooms did not obey the law of total tricks—another 1993 Bols Tip. "Always lead your singleton"—an earlier Bols Tip—semi-exposed the shape and honour cards in West. My 1993 Bols Tip of hiding a key queen might have helped. West displayed her highest cards at every opportunity to hide the crucial queen of hearts. Take the spade with the queen. Confidently lead the king of diamonds instead of the jack. These "seeking" plays portrayed a holding of ♠KQ and ◊KQ with West. The backward finesse in trumps would appear less attractive. Given the bidding and play, these Queen-Hiding manoeuvres should not distract partner. Declarer might still prevail, but West would be unimpeachable after using three Bols Tips, even if unknowingly.

An innocent queen

2002 Far East and Pacific
Bridge Championship
Youth: Hong Kong v Australia
S/ EW vulnerable

	♠ 63	
	♡ AJ852	
	◊ J2	
	♣ AK98	
♠ 852		♠ A1097
♡ Q10		♡ 974
◊ A109876		◊ 5
♣ 75		♣ Q10642
	♠ KQJ4	
	♡ K63	
	◊ KQ43	
	♣ J3	

A Queen Drop is not a joke. As observed in recent prestigious tournaments, defenders treasure their queens, declining to discard the queen from QJ10x to inform partner of a timely shift, or to make a Queen Sacrifice requesting partner to switch to beat a contract. This hand was an easy 3NT or 4♡. If defenders did not find the ruff in diamonds, declarer took eleven tricks for 450.

The Australian Moscito bidding system placed South as the declarer in 4♡. West was L H Chin. He led the seven of clubs to dummy's ace. Declarer led to the king of hearts. Chin innocently and smoothly dropped the queen. The apparently short club and singleton heart placed Chin with length in spades and diamonds. Declarer looked to lose two aces and a trump. If declarer established the side suits, he risked defensive ruffs. If he drew trumps, he might be forced in clubs and have to scramble to make his contract.

It seemed safe to ruff clubs in hand with the short trumps. Declarer cashed the king of clubs and ruffed a club, snatching a defeat from the jaws of victory. Chin overruffed, cashed the ace of diamonds, and returned a diamond. East ruffed and cashed the ace of spades to score down one, plus 50. When declarer played the king, Chin knew of his Doomed Queen from the ♡AJ of hearts in dummy. My 1993 Bols Tip recommended dropping the doomed queen early as a camouflage to test declarer. It took nine years for the Tip to be duplicated by my compatriot and reported in an international bulletin.

A glamorous queen

	♠ KJ1076	
2008 Yeh Brothers Cup	♡ K98	
South Africa v USA	◇ AQ	
E/ EW vulnerable	♣ K93	

	♠ A98		♠ Q54
	♡ Q542		♡ 1076
	◇ J864		◇ 107532
	♣ A5		♣ Q10

	♠ 32	
	♡ AJ3	
	◇ K9	
	♣ J87642	

West	North	East	South
Bosenberg	Hampson	Eber	Kranyak
Pass	1NT	Pass	3♣*
Pass	3♠ (5-card)	Pass	3NT

*Stayman for 5-card major

This Queen Drop occurred in a world event with hefty cash prizes. Many at South played 3NT, concealing the club suit. Hampson of USA, a 2010 Rosenblum Cup winner, declared 3NT as North after a 1NT opening with a five-card major. His opponents were Eber and Bosenberg, South African stars who eliminated Italy in the 2007 Bermuda Bowl. Eber, as East, led a small diamond to the king in dummy and the queen in declarer. West played the eight, suggesting a four-card suit. East knew that declarer had five spades and two diamonds and therefore held at least three clubs.

Declarer led a club to his king. Eber, well prepared, smoothly followed with the queen of clubs. He knew from the play at the first trick that maintaining the lead in dummy but exposing AQ doubleton in declarer would be sensible only with an impending club lead. A further implication was that West had the ace of clubs. The fate of his queen was doomed as he also possessed the ten. After the camouflage drop of the Bols Tip queen of clubs, it was not attractive for declarer to continue clubs. Fact trumped fiction. Declarer switched to the finesse of a heart to the jack, followed by finessing a spade to another jack, an anti-percentage play. When West took the jack with the queen of hearts and continued a diamond; declarer crossed to the ace of hearts for the finesse in spades. The result was down three, minus 150.

Eber dressed up his queen, playing it in tempo, so that declarer diverted his attention to the other suits. In old civilizations, kings donated their glamorous beauties to become queens of enemies, thereby securing peace. Eber saved his kingdom with his glamorous queen.

Fortune transformation

2001 Polish open team	♠ KQJ5		
W/ Neither vulnerable	♡ A5		
	◊ AJ742		
	♣ A5		

West		East
♠ A1094		♠ 872
♡ KQ1094		♡ 62
◊ Q9		◊ 1086
♣ 74		♣ K10982

	♠ 63
	♡ J873
	◊ K53
	♣ QJ63

West	North	East	South
Latala	Siwiec	Kwiecien	Tuszynski
1♡	Double	Pass	1NT
Pass	3NT		

By now, the Doomed Queen and the Queen Sacrifice are familiar. Latala, as West, led the king of hearts. Declarer was World Olympiad champion in 1984. He won with dummy's ace and played spades. West ducked the king and took the queen with his ace. He continued with the ten of spades to the jack. Declarer returned to hand with the king of diamonds. Latala followed with the queen, a Queen Drop.

To a world champion, the solution was deceptively simple. West had to be 4-6-1-2 with the king of clubs. Declarer planned to finesse a club through West and cash the ace of clubs and ◊AJ to confirm the Queen Drop. The fourth spade endplayed West. West had to lead hearts. The jack of hearts was the ninth trick.

The subtlety was that declarer was in hand and had no more entries. He had to take the finesse now. When the queen lost to the king of clubs in East, the return of a heart allowed West to take two tricks, and the fourth spade sunk the contract for 50. The Bols Tip succeeded again. By dropping his queen early and smoothly, Latala transformed his doomed queen into the doomed play by a world champion

Reversing an endplay

2003 USA Fall National
Team Championship
E/ Neither vulnerable

	♠ AKJ86	
	♡ 942	
	◊ 10	
	♣ KJ96	
♠ Q5		♠ 10973
♡ AQ7		♡ 105
◊ K9875		◊ J43
♣ 542		♣ Q1083
	♠ 42	
	♡ KJ863	
	◊ AQ62	
	♣ A7	

West	*North*	*East*	*South*
Rao	Bocchi	Humphries	Duboin
		Pass	1♡
Pass	1NT (5+♠)	Pass	2◊ (less than 3♠)
Pass	4♡		

If you think that Bols Tip lightning does not strike twice, this episode proves otherwise. The bidding represents the new wave of the responder-transfer bid. Its gain in popularity reflects its distracting effect on opponents. However, here it was Rao who distracted declarer Duboin.

Rao led the five of clubs to the king in dummy. Declarer crossed to his ace of diamonds and ruffed a diamond in dummy. He returned to his ace of clubs for a second ruff in diamonds. Rao must have been concentrating. When declarer next played the ace of spades, Rao dropped his queen nonchalantly. Declarer took stock and led the nine of clubs. This was fatal without cashing the king of spades.

East was probably from the same school. He false-carded with the queen of clubs. Declarer ruffed in hand and played his remaining diamond, ruffed in dummy, and was overruffed by East with the ten. East returned his fourth club. Declarer had ♠4 ♡KJ86. West had ♠5 ♡AQ7 ◇9. East's remaining trump was ♡5. Declarer had to ruff with the eight, and West discarded a spade. Declarer played the king of hearts to the ace. Rao led a diamond, forcing declarer to ruff. His ♡Q7 took two tricks for down one.

If Rao does not play the Queen Drop on the first spade, declarer cashes the king, ruffs a club, and ruffs a diamond. East overruffs. When East leads a club, declarer has ♡KJ86, West has ♡AQ7 ◇9, and East's trump holding is ♡5. Declarer ruffs with the eight. If West discards, declarer plays the king of hearts and West is endplayed. If West overruffs, he is also endplayed.

Rao resourcefully used his the Doomed Queen of spades to derail declarer. In the 2009 Bermuda Bowl, Duboin bowed to another Queen Drop when he cashed a singleton side ace in dummy. He adopted an alternative line and failed in a slam. The defender won the best defence of the year award. He was Askari of Pakistan, who dropped his queen from ◇Q52.

A fifth dimension

	♠ AKJ652		
2004 USA Fall National	♡ Q763		
Spingold knock-out teams	◊ 7		
S/ Neither vulnerable	♣ 76		

♠ Q107		♠ 983
♡ K82		♡ 95
◊ Q9853		◊ A1064
♣ 94		♣ AKJ5

	♠ 4	
	♡ AJ104	
	◊ KJ2	
	♣ Q10832	

West	*North*	*East*	*South*
Levit			
Pass	Pass	Pass	1♣
Pass	1♠	Pass	2♣
Pass	3♠	Pass	3NT

This hand shows a Queen Defence. The event was Spingold. Matches were tight. This explained the play of this hand in both rooms. In the first room, East took the lead of a diamond with the ace and returned a diamond to the jack and queen. Taking the diamond return with the king, declarer finessed spades. After cashing the spades and observing the defence signals, declarer abandoned the finesse in hearts. He was correct: down only one.

In the other room, the bidding was the same. Levit, sitting West, also led a diamond to the ace but ducked the jack on the return, a camouflage hiding his queen and sacrificing a trick. Declarer could finesse the queen of spades to arrive at nine tricks. Under the impression that West held good clubs when he chose to lead a paltry suit—and that therefore East held the queen of spades—declarer led to the king of spades and passed the queen of hearts to the king. Levit continued a diamond, resulting in down two, plus 2 IMPs. His team won by 1 IMP.

Levit knew his queen of spades was doomed. He sacrificed and camouflaged at the second trick, hiding two queens in a single move: a Bols Tip in a fifth dimension. He traded a magnificent diamond trick for four spade tricks.

Dancing queen

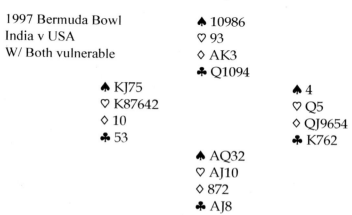

1997 Bermuda Bowl
India v USA
W/ Both vulnerable

```
                    ♠ 10986
                    ♡ 93
                    ◊ AK3
                    ♣ Q1094
        ♠ KJ75                      ♠ 4
        ♡ K87642                    ♡ Q5
        ◊ 10                        ◊ QJ9654
        ♣ 53                        ♣ K762
                    ♠ AQ32
                    ♡ AJ10
                    ◊ 872
                    ♣ AJ8
```

Having a doubleton queen, defenders know when to play the queen on the first round to force a premature honour from declarer. "Rectifying the count" is a familiar bridge term. At most tables, South opened 1NT and declared 4♠ via Stayman. West led his singleton diamond, taken by dummy's king. Declarer passed the ten of spades to the jack. West returned a club to the nine. East played small. The queen of clubs was led from dummy. East ducked, preserving his king. Declarer continued a spade to his queen and the king. West returned a spade to dummy's nine. Next was a heart played to the jack. The position was now as follows:

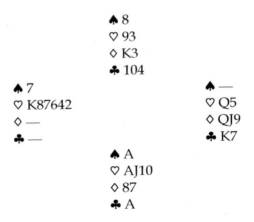

After taking the trick with the king of hearts, any return from West would squeeze East in the minors. When declarer cashed the hearts and the trump, dummy discarded a diamond. East had to unguard a minor. Declarer cashed the minor that East unguarded and scored 620 in a crisscross squeeze.

West should therefore duck the heart. If declarer drew trumps and played a small heart, East would take with his queen and return a minor to break up the squeeze. If declarer played a small heart, East could return a minor for West to ruff. If declarer cashed his ace of hearts, ruffed a heart, and led a club from dummy, West would ruff and play the king of hearts. Dummy had to discard before East. If declarer led a diamond instead of a club, East would take the trick, giving West a ruff.

If East rose with a Queen-Seeking heart in the diagrammed position, and declarer took with his ace and played a heart, West should still duck. Declarer could not cash the spade before playing a heart to squeeze East, because this would allow West the rest of the tricks. If he ruffed a heart in dummy, the defence would succeed along the line just described.

The difficulty was detecting declarer's layout and the rectification of count. East should play the queen of hearts. Seeing the dancing queen, West could envision declarer's hand and defend accordingly. No team found the defence.

The great pretender

Kaplan Coup
N/ Neither vulnerable

```
                    ♠ 93
                    ♡ AQ
                    ◊ AQ10764
                    ♣ 1098
  ♠ 1042                           ♠ AK865
  ♡ J108532                        ♡ 74
  ◊ J3                             ◊ 95
  ♣ A5                             ♣ KJ74
                    ♠ QJ7
                    ♡ K96
                    ◊ K82
                    ♣ Q632
```

West	North	East	South
		Kaplan	
	1◊	1♠	1NT
2♡	3◊	Pass	3NT

It takes more than skill to extract a treasured queen. Kaplan's articles in *The Bridge World* set a standard difficult to surmount. This was one of his nirvanas. You would agree that 3NT was a leisurely stroll. Kaplan showed otherwise.

Taking the deuce of spades lead with the king, Kaplan deliberated. His partner did not support spades. There was little prospect in that suit. Red finesses seemed charmingly positioned for declarer. Hearts and diamonds were ripe for at least eight tricks. The ♣1098 in dummy were tall stewards guarding against unwelcome visitors. Declarer had apparently a complete queen collection. It was frustrating.

Kaplan decided to change destiny. He tabled the king of clubs with the sublime manner of one also holding the ace. His partner played small, sensing that Kaplan had the ace of spades as an entry if required. When Kaplan next distributed a small club, declarer confidently rose with the queen. A delighted West accepted with his ace. Kaplan greeted the second spade with his ace, followed by the mercurial and triumphant jack of clubs. The precious seven of clubs was a bonus for the ceremony, down two and 100.

A real and sham sacrifice

IBPA defence of the year: 2010	♠ 5432		
2009 Bermuda Bowl	♡ AK754		
Italy v Pakistan	◇ Q52		
W/ EW vulnerable	♣ 9		

```
                    ♠ AQJ10          ♠ K9876
                    ♡ 3              ♡ 1086
                    ◇ KJ9764         ◇ A
                    ♣ 74             ♣ AK102

                         ♠ —
                         ♡ QJ92
                         ◇ 1083
                         ♣ QJ8653
```

West	North	East	South
Duboin	Askari	Sementa	Mohinddin
1◇	1♡	Double (4+♠)	4♡
4♠	Pass	5♣ (control)	Pass
5◇	Pass	5NT	Pass
6♠			

When Netherlands played USA2, they went down in 6♠. Stewart led the ♡AK. After ruffing the second heart, declarer Bakkeren tried the ace of diamonds, ♣AK, intending to crossruff for twelve tricks. When Stewart ruffed the second club it was down one, minus 100. His teammates sacrificed in 7♡, minus 1400. Declarer would have fared better if he had drawn a trump after the ace of diamonds, played the king of diamonds, ruffed a diamond, played a trump to hand, led the good diamonds, overruffing

North as necessary, and returned to hand to draw trumps, scoring 1430.

The Chinese Taipei South was on lead playing Germany. Her partner overtook the lead of queen of hearts and returned a club to the ace. Declarer cashed his ace of diamonds, led a spade to the ten, ruffed a diamond, and returned a spade to the queen. He ruffed another diamond establishing the suit, drew the remaining trumps, and claimed as the diamonds were good.

The play therefore depends on an evaluation of the lengths of the minors in North. The 1993 Bols Tip advised a nonchalant, smooth dropping of a doomed queen to steer declarer away from the winning play—not obvious here. In the diagrammed deal, Askari, as North, led the ace of hearts and a small heart. Duboin tested the waters by playing the ace of clubs and the ace of diamonds. Askari smoothly dropped the queen.

West, many times world champion, thought it safe to cash the king of clubs, as North would not have two singletons based on the bidding. Askari ruffed to defeat the contract. He knew his queen of diamonds would be doomed in three rounds and dropped it earliest. For his insight, Askari received the best defence award from the International Bridge Press Association in 2010. For Duboin, it was a second lightning strike, as he had bowed to a Queen Drop in 2003. As for Italy, they lost the final to USA.

This hand demonstrates a Queen Drop to distract declarer from ruffing out his long suit. In the 2011 China Elite tournament, no international experts attempted a similar award-winning Drop to test declarer in a 4♠ contract.

7

QUEEN PLAY

TIPS FOR
Queen Play

- ♛ Organise a ruffing plan.
- ♛ Play a queen in the jack doubleton suit of opponents when endplayed.
- ♛ Discover a crucial queen from a busy defender.
- ♛ Discover a crucial queen from an opening lead.
- ♛ Discover a crucial trump by playing side suits.
- ♛ Disturb a discovery play of a declarer.
- ♛ Discover a winning line without locating a crucial queen.

This chapter features enhanced versions of my 1993 Bols Tip. It begins with Queen-Seeking hands, an entry blocking queen play by defenders, similar to the sham queen sacrifice in chess. As an example dummy has J9 trumps and you have queen fifth behind declarer. The only defence is to play the queen. Queen and Jack Discovery follow. The chapter concludes with an example in which declarer did not need a Queen Discovery for a slam.

Queen play

Play skillfully
with your
queens.

Queen play

A philosophical queen

1998 India	♠ KJ632
National Team championship	♡ KQ65
E/ Both vulnerable	◇ J3
	♣ 65

	♠ Q10754		♠ A8
	♡ J102		♡ A9873
	◇ 72		◇ Q85
	♣ 984		♣ K107

| ♠ 9 |
| ♡ 4 |
| ◇ AK10964 |
| ♣ AQJ32 |

West	North	East	South
		Datar	
		1♡	2NT (minors)
Pass	3NT	Pass	5◇

    Queening defence varies. In chess, a sham queen sacrifice is a tactic to win the game. This bridge hand represents this approach. West led the jack of hearts to dummy's queen and East's ace. Datar sat East. He cashed the ace of spades. West gave count. Datar judged from the bidding and play that declarer held a 1-1-6-5 shape. His hand was also an open book for declarer. Datar's return presented declarer with a trick in the majors or a finesse in the minors. Declarer finessed his king of clubs, cashed the ace, and ruffed a club. With a friendly break in clubs, declarer finessed trumps to score 600.

Datar sacrificed his ◇Q. It was the only defence. Declarer took the trick and went to dummy with the ◇J, pitched two clubs with his kings in the majors, and finessed clubs once. He lost to the king of clubs for down one. The ◇Q eliminated a ruff and an entry in dummy, where the sole entry was now the ◇J. There was no defense against the philosophical queen, a sham queen sacrifice.

A sham queen sacrifice

		♠ 6	
2009		♡ KQ75	
World Transnational Team		◇ J8642	
S/ EW vulnerable		♣ K104	

	♠ J9		♠ AK1054
	♡ AJ83		♡ 10
	◇ 9		◇ K10753
	♣ Q98632		♣ AJ

		♠ Q8732	
		♡ 9642	
		◇ AQ	
		♣ 75	

West	North	East	South
	Robinson		Boyd
			Pass
Pass	Pass	1♠	Pass
1NT	Double	2◇	2♡
2♠	3♡	3♠	

An invincible queen sacrifice of the Datar type resurfaced eleven years later in an international bridge bulletin. South led a heart against 3♠, to dummy's ace. A diamond was led to the king and ace. An exit of a club from South presented a free finesse. An exit in hearts would be ruffed by declarer. Declarer ruffed a diamond, finessed a club, cashed his ace of clubs, and played a diamond. South had to step up with the ♠Q; otherwise, dummy would ruff. A heart was ruffed in hand, and the ♠AK fulfilled the contract for 140. After his ♠Q, South was able to return a spade to dummy's ♠J. Declarer ruffed a heart in hand. With the ♠AK10, there were nine tricks. An exit in diamonds led to a similar play and the same results. An exit of a trump would be taken by dummy's nine.

Declarer finessed a club to his jack, cashed the ace of clubs, ruffed a diamond, and ruffed a heart. He had six tricks and ♠AK10 left. South had four trumps left and would be end-played to lead into declarer's tenace. Boyd found the Queen Defence, the ♠Q. Declarer gratefully won with the ace, ruffed a diamond, finessed a club, cashed the club ace, and played a diamond.

The difference was that declarer had ♠K1054. South had ♠8732. North took two diamonds and led a diamond. Boyd ruffed small and returned a heart. His remaining spades were good spot cards for down one and 100. The Queen Defence eliminated a ruff and an entry to dummy. Unlike Datar's Doomed Queen, Boyd's queen was more charming, sitting behind the king. Declarer could succeed if he finessed a club at the second trick, cashed the ace of clubs, and floated a low diamond.

A lonely jack

	♠ A2		
2001 Bermuda Bowl final	♡ J97		
USA v Norway	◊ J9		
W/ Both vulnerable	♣ KJ7654		

♠ 1065	♠ KQ8
♡ Q1043	♡ A82
◊ 10654	◊ Q83
♣ 109	♣ Q832

	♠ J9743
	♡ K65
	◊ AK72
	♣ A

West Sontag	North Saelensminde	East Weichsel	South Brogeland
Pass	1♣	Pass	1♠
Pass	2♣	Pass	2◊
Pass	3♣	Pass	3NT

Helgemo	Martel	Helness	Stansby
Pass	Pass	1♣	1♠
Pass	1NT	Pass	2◊
Pass	2♠		

The diamonds in North looked familiar. After an initial Pass by North, USA2 in the second room bid and made 2♠. In the first room, West led a heart to the ace against 3NT. East returned a heart to the queen when declarer ducked. Knowing his lack of entries, West switched to a spade. East took the spade with the queen and continued spades. Declarer was Brogeland. He took the trick with the ace, crossed to the ace of clubs, cashed the king of hearts, and advanced the jack of spades to the king. East was endplayed, having only minors left.

East returned a low diamond. Declarer passed to dummy's jack, cashed the king of clubs, and returned to hand to cash his winners in diamonds and spades. He scored 600. Despite losing this hand, USA2 won the final.

East missed a sham queen sacrifice. He had thirteen high-card points. His partner should not have more than a queen. Declarer therefore held the top diamonds. Based on the play, his partner was likely to be 3-4-4-2. Declarer held one club, and it was the ace. The evaluation matched the play, testing the broken spades rather than the long clubs. The ◊J9 in dummy looked familiar. Play the ◊Q. Taking the queen with his king and cashing spades, declarer could not cash the ◊A without smothering the lonely ◊J in dummy. If he crossed to the ◊J, he could not score his ◊A. East missed an opportunity to join Datar and Boyd in finding a distinguished and unbeatable Queen Defence.

A little bit of help

2005 Denmark	♠ A1053		
Hecht Cup	♡ A85		
E/ Neither vulnerable	◊ Q7		
	♣ 9752		

♠ J982			♠ Q76
♡ 74			♡ Q63
◊ K854			◊ AJ92
♣ AQ4			♣ 863

	♠ K4		
	♡ KJ1092		
	◊ 1063		
	♣ KJ10		

West	North	East	South
Hagen	Blasket	Larsen	Hecht-Johansen
		Pass	1♡
Pass	1♠	Pass	2♣
Pass	3♡		

We turn to the technique of Queen Discovery. This hand is from a tournament modeled on the Cavendish pairs, which features an auction pool. Most tables played 3♥ and many received a trump lead. At this table, declarer welcomed the small trump lead. He let it run to his nine and advanced a diamond. West rose with the king and returned a second trump to the eight. Declarer finessed a club to the queen. West returned a diamond to the ace. East continued a trump. Declarer lost three diamonds and two clubs for down one, minus 50.

At another table Fredin received the same lead of a trump. He learned two messages: (1) the defence would draw three rounds of trumps, denying dummy a ruff and (2) this was an opportunity for Queen Discovery. East held three trumps with the queen. He played the ace and led a club to his jack and the queen. East gave count. West led a second trump. Declarer took the trick and played the king of clubs, establishing the suit. As the fourth club in dummy provided a discard of a diamond loser, declarer lost only two diamonds, making 140. A little bit of help from the opening lead enlightened declarer to a winning path.

A busy defender

2006 China
National open teams
S/ NS vulnerable

♠ AK85
♡ K82
◇ 6
♣ K10943

♠ J9
♡ AQ9
◇ QJ105
♣ Q852

♠ Q743
♡ J10643
◇ 82
♣ 76

♠ 1062
♡ 75
◇ AK9743
♣ AJ

West	North	East	South
Shi	Fu	Zhuang	Zhao
			1◇
Pass	2♣	Pass	2◇
Pass	2♠	Pass	3◇
Pass	3NT		

This hand features Queen Hiding and Seeking. Declarer had an additional task of locating an ace. North-South won the World Open Pairs and the Vanderbilt in 2006. East and West were national team regulars.

East led a small heart, the unbid suit. West played the queen. Declarer had nine tricks if he guessed the queen of clubs and clubs broke evenly. As assessed by Fu, the chance was slim. Fu decided to play West for the ace of hearts and ducked the queen. West shifted to an entry-disrupting jack of diamonds. Declarer played the ace and led a heart. West surfaced with his ace of hearts and switched to the nine of spades.

At the other tables, declarer scored nine tricks easily after ducking the heart lead and driving out the queen of clubs. After this defence, declarer should still make his contract, but there were ways to go down. If declarer played the king of spades and finessed to the jack of clubs, and West continued spades, the contract failed. The industrious defence of West exposed his short majors and long minors. Fu decided to play West for four clubs with the queen. He cashed the ♠AK, king of hearts, and ace of clubs, and passed the jack of clubs. West ducked. Declarer cashed the king of diamonds and played a diamond. West took two diamond tricks but had to lead clubs into declarer's tenace. The spectacular play won Fu the 2006 Xin Hua award in China for the best declarer play. West had orchestrated a symphony but missed a crucial musical note: the hiding of the queen of clubs. The Bols Tip would recommend playing the ◊Q instead of the ◊J, and returning a third round of hearts instead of starting spades.

A bachelor king

2008 Olympiad
Ladies team quarterfinal
China v Germany
N/ Neither vulnerable

	♠ J1062	
	♡ 984	
	◊ 103	
	♣ Q654	
♠ KQ873		♠ —
♡ KJ75		♡ A632
◊ A52		◊ KQJ64
♣ 10		♣ AJ92
	♠ A954	
	♡ Q10	
	◊ 987	
	♣ K873	

West	North	East	South
H L Wang	Auken	Sun	von Armin
	Pass	1◊	Pass
1♠	Pass	2♡	Pass
4♣	Pass	4◊	Pass
4NT	Pass	6♡	

Not all hands require Queen Discovery. This was the first hand of the last session in a tight match. The other room played 4♡. China bid to a slam. If South led a diamond, declarer won and passed the king of spades to the ace. Winning the return, declarer would finesse a heart to the jack, ruff a spade, cash the ♡AK, cross to diamonds to discard two spades, and land twelve tricks for 980. This line of play required either the spade or the heart finesse to be right.

Sun did not attempt to seek the queen of trumps for her bachelor king. This required a non-diamond lead. Based on the bidding, South led a low club to the ace. Declarer ruffed a club in dummy, led the king of spades and ruffed. She ruffed a club, crossed to the king of diamonds, led her fourth club, ruffing with dummy's jack, cashed the king of hearts, crossed to the queen of diamonds, and played the ace of hearts. On this trick, Sun discarded the ace of diamonds, an Emperor's coup. She ran the diamonds. North could take her third trump when she wanted. Sun had long trumps in her hand to take care of any return. The Queen Play brought 11 IMPs. China won and beat USA in the semifinal. They lost by 1 IMP to England in the final.

A psychic and a mathematician

		♠ K75432	
2008 European Cup		♡ AJ	
Germany v Poland		◊ AK7	
Norway v Russia		♣ KQ	
E/ NS vulnerable	♠ —		♠ AJ6
	♡ 10987		♡ Q43
	◊ Q10654		◊ J82
	♣ 10982		♣ J753
		♠ Q1098	
		♡ K652	
		◊ 93	
		♣ A64	

West	North	East	South
		Norway v Russia	
Lund	Khiouppenen	Helgemo	Kholomeev
		Pass	Pass
2◊ (weak)	Double	Redouble	Pass
2♡	2♠	Pass	4♠
	Poland v Germany		
Gierulski	Gromoeller	Skrzypczak	Kirmse
		Pass	Pass
1◊	Double	1NT	2◊
Pass	4♠		

Finding a jack can be fun or agony. Almost all tables bid 6♠. Norway and Poland attempted a psychic opening by West, a third-seat non-vulnerable gambit deployed by some experts. Their opponents missed the slam. There were similar results at other tables.

In another room, Russia's West passed in his first round, and North declared 6♠. A club was led. Molberg of Norway, the eventual champion team, won in hand. He thought it straightforward to draw trumps by delivering a spade towards the queen. Jagniewski of Poland did the same. Both went down, losing two trumps to the ♠AJ6, an 11% chance. Their natural hand movements, repeated by numerous other declarers, frustrated the psychic bids of their teammates. If the diagrammed tables reached the slam, declarers should succeed, smelling spade shortage in West.

There was a left-hander. Bompis of France played the king of spades without any bidding clues. He inferred from the lead that East had a balanced hand. There was no report of declarers attempting a Jack Discovery. The percentage of a singleton diamond was about 3%. A mathematician would cash the top diamonds before touching trumps. When the second diamond dropped an eight from East, declarer would play the king of spades first. The risk was that West would have ♠J6 and doubleton diamonds. A diamond through dummy after the ace of spades would promote the jack, or vice versa—about a 2% chance. However, a mundane West might accidentally drop a psychic queen or ten on the second diamond, the Bols Tip. This attracted declarer to play a spade to his queen. A psychic drop would defeat a dedicated mathematician.

8

TRUMP SOLDIERS

We conclude with defence with trump strengths. Trumps include KJ107 and J10432 against slams, QJ42 and KJ93 against games, and Q74 and Q92 against slams. Defenders had to play hide-and-seek with declarer. In one hand, the defender had to contribute his queen of trumps from a three-card holding to beat the slam. In "Sleeping With Your Enemy," the sole question for defenders was whether or not to cover with their trump honour. The hands illustrate that while no formula is available, clues often emerge. The book ends with "A Submarine in Heaven," a slam where the only defence was a divine duck of a jack.

A beloved lady

2001 USA Fall National		♠ 43	
Open pairs		♡ J62	
S/ Both vulnerable		♦ 542	
		♣ QJ1062	

♠ 10962			♠ Q7
♡ 10			♡ Q874
♦ Q8763			♦ KJ9
♣ 983			♣ K754

		♠ AKJ85	
		♡ AK953	
		♦ A10	
		♣ A	

West	*North*	*East*	*South*
			2♣ (strong)
Pass	2♦ (relay)	Pass	2♠
Pass	3♣ (weak)	Pass	3♡
Pass	3♠	Pass	5♡

This chapter describes hands with good trumps. Naturally, the trump queen plays a prominent role. This hand is about queen hiding. A natural sequence resulted in an embarrassing five-level contract. West inserted the jack on partner's low diamond lead. Declarer ducked. East continued diamonds to the ace. Declarer cashed the ace and king of spades, and ace of hearts, noting the ten from West. He led a small spade and ruffed with the jack in dummy.

East counted on declarer having 5-5 in the majors and two minor-suit aces, to justify his aggressiveness. An overruff would unlikely gain. His remaining ♡87 would be easy meat for the ♡K9 of declarer. Defenders needed two more tricks. East's ♡Q87 figured to score at least a trick. Declarer might need to ruff a spade loser in dummy. East could decline to overruff.

Having concentrated before the first trick, East discarded a club under the jack of hearts smoothly and quickly. Declarer played a heart to his king to drop the presumed doubleton-queen; otherwise, a further spade from West would promote a trump trick for East. He lost two hearts, conceding 100. East shielded his beloved lady from an unwelcome pursuit. He did it with foresight on a fast track.

Lonely jack versus lonely queen

1999 Netherlands	♠ —
Cap Gemini pairs	♡ 53
W/ NS vulnerable	◊ KJ43
	♣ AJ109852

	♠ KQ97654		♠ AJ83
	♡ Q		♡ 109764
	◊ Q92		◊ 7
	♣ 76		♣ KQ4

	♠ 102
	♡ AKJ82
	◊ A10865
	♣ 3

West	North	East	South
Versace	Justin Hackett	Lauria	Jason Hackett
3♠	4♣	4♠	4NT
Pass	5♣	Pass	5◊
Pass	6◊		

Westerhof	Helness	Jansen	Helgemo
3♠	4♣	4♠	Double
Pass	4NT	Pass	6◊

This hand was a game of hide-and-seek with queens. The occasion was an annual pairs event. The organizers invited three Netherlands pairs and thirteen international pairs to compete for trophies and cash prizes.

Many tables reached a slam. At the first table, declarer ruffed the king of spades lead. He played a heart to his ace, dropping the queen. It seemed appropriate to establish clubs. The ace of clubs and a club ruff revealed a 3-2 break. East dropped his king. South thought of playing two rounds of trumps. If trumps break evenly, a second club ruff would establish the suit. Dummy still had a trump to enjoy the clubs for thirteen tricks. The danger was a 3-1 break in trumps. There would be inadequate entries to run the clubs.

If declarer ruffs his last spade in dummy and ruffs a club back small, an overruff by West would be welcome. Declarer would take the spade return in hand, play two rounds of trumps, ending in dummy, and run the clubs. West should therefore discard instead of overruffing. If declarer plays a winning heart, again West should discard. Declarer ruffed a heart with the ◊J in dummy, played the ◊K, and led a winning club, discarding a heart loser. West could ruff at the expense of his trump trick. Helgemo adopted this successful line at the second table.

At the first table, declarer played the ◊K after the club ruff. This was fatal. He ruffed the third club with his ◊10. Versace, as West, refused to overruff with his ◊Q, eloquently pitching a spade. Otherwise, the ◊J4 in dummy could ruff a spade return small, allowing declarer to draw trumps with the jack and claim. Declarer tried the jack of hearts. West ruffed. He forced dummy with a spade. The lone ◊J in dummy could not draw the lone ◊Q in West. Dummy had to play a club. After a short wait, Versace ruffed with his queen punctually to defeat the contract.

An arithmetic subtraction

```
1991 USA                      ♠ A432
Vanderbilt knock-out teams    ♡ A76
N/ NS vulnerable              ◊ K94
                              ♣ K53

        ♠ Q1065                           ♠ KJ987
        ♡ J8542                           ♡ K103
        ◊ 5                               ◊ QJ103
        ♣ Q74                             ♣ 8

                              ♠ —
                              ♡ Q9
                              ◊ A8762
                              ♣ AJ10962
```

West	North	East	South
			Cohen
	1NT (14-16)	2♡ (♠+minor)	3♠ (short)
Double	3NT	Pass	4♣
Pass	4♠	Pass	6♣

Finding a defender with queen third in trumps is only part of the job. This hand is about Queen Seeking. West led a diamond to the ace. Declarer returned a diamond. West declined to ruff, discarding a heart. The king in dummy took the trick. If declarer played a third round of diamonds, a continuation by East would be ruffed by West with a trump higher than the five, forcing the king. The contract failed when West had three trumps with the queen.

Cohen found a Queen Play based on the competitive bidding. He ruffed a small spade in hand and launched the nasty nine of clubs, passing through West. Only then did he play a diamond. East took the trick. On a diamond continuation, West did force the king of clubs with his seven. However, the ace later swallowed his lone queen for 1370.

The bidding and play should also inform West of the distributions in the minors, and the need of a diamond ruff in dummy. A Queen Discovery of the trumps should not escape an expert declarer, who would envision an uneven break in trumps and finesse the queen through West. The queen of clubs was functionally a Doomed Queen. West should therefore consider covering the nasty nine with his queen. Importantly, after chewing the queen with the king, the ♣53 in dummy could not overruff West's ♣74. After passing the ♣9, West had ♣Q7, which could not force the ♣K5 in dummy without losing his queen. It was an exercise in simple arithmetic subtraction.

Patience

2009 Venice Cup final	♠ K1062
China v USA	♡ J
E/ Both vulnerable	◇ 864
	♣ AQ852

♠ Q75		♠ A984
♡ 74		♡ KQ9653
◇ AJ53		◇ 109
♣ J763		♣ 4

	♠ J3
	♡ A1082
	◇ KQ72
	♣ K109

West	North	East	South
Sun	Levitina	H L Wang	Sanborn
		1♡	Pass
1NT	Pass	2♡	Pass
Pass	Double	Pass	3◇

We continue the theme of defenders possessing good trumps. West held a Bath coup combination of trumps. In the other room, Liu and W F Wang of China defended 2♥, down two, plus 200. In the Bermuda Bowl final, 3◊ scored 110. West took the first round of trumps with the ace. Declarer drew one more round. He had three clubs, one trick each in the other suits, a heart ruff, and a spade ruff. As West had four clubs, declarer could ruff the fourth club for his ninth trick.

In this room, Sun led a heart to the queen and ace. Declarer led a spade to the ten and ace. East returned a spade to the jack, queen, and king. Declarer led a diamond to the king. Sun ducked. This was the key patience play, a Bath coup variation.

Declarer ruffed a heart in dummy. If she drew a trump to the queen, West would play two rounds and press declarer to ruff a spade. On reflection, West did not bid 1♠ or support hearts, or give East a club ruff. West was probably 3-2-4-4, which fit with 4-6-2-1 of East. Declarer should guess the layout of the clubs, scoring 110.

Declarer, not wanting to waste the remaining trump in dummy, led a club to her king for another heart ruff. West discarded a spade. The play of the ace of clubs was fatal, as East ruffed, cashed her king of hearts, and led a spade. West overruffed the ◊2 with her ◊5. West continued a club, and her ◊AJ scored the last two tricks for 200. China defeated USA for their first women's crown.

Sleeping with your enemy

2005 Australia
National teams
S/ Neither vulnerable

	♠ 4	
	♡ A986	
	◊ AQJ8	
	♣ 9654	

♠ 108763		♠ Q2
♡ KJ742		♡ Q53
◊ 72		◊ 10965
♣ 3		♣ KJ107

	♠ AKJ95	
	♡ 10	
	◊ K43	
	♣ AQ82	

West	North	East	South
	Lester		Bourke
			1♠
Pass	2◊	Pass	3♣
Pass	3♡	Pass	4◊
Pass	6♣		

One should never complain about defending a slam with KJ107 of trumps. This hand describes classic finesses holding AQ98. West led a heart, the fourth suit bid by dummy. Bourke declared. He put up the ace from dummy and led a small club to the eight. After cashing the ace of spades and ruffing a spade, he led a second club to his queen and ruffed a second spade with the nine. East had ♣KJ; declarer had ♣A2. If East overruffed, Bourke could win or ruff the return, draw the remaining trump in East, and claim. If East declined to ruff, declarer could play out his spade and diamond winners until East did ruff. Declarer was in command with the ace of clubs.

A club to the eight was entirely proper, catering to ♣J10 in East. East slept with his enemy. He should have inserted the ten on the first trump. Declarer covered with his queen, played the ace of spades, ruffed a spade, and led a club. East inserted his jack. Declarer covered with the ace and ruffed a second spade high. East had ♣K7 and declarer had ♣82. East discarded a diamond. If declarer played four rounds of diamonds, East would discard a heart. Declarer had only hearts in dummy. He would have to force himself on the next heart, and East would take the last tricks, a reverse trump coup. If declarer ruffed a heart and played four rounds of diamonds, East would ruff the fourth round with the king and play a heart. Declarer would have to ruff with his remaining trump. East's fourth trump would sink the slam.

The clue was an entry to force declarer in hearts. The trump insertions allowed East to ruff high with his third trump. His fourth trump would score after forcing declarer. If declarer adopted the alternative, the trump insertions reversed the trump coup. East would be in command instead of declarer. By analyzing the flow of the play, East could have decided to split his trump honours. East slept and waited in vain.

A stripping chase

2008 USA
Open team trials
N/ Both vulnerable

♠ Q642
♡ 4
◇ AKQ85
♣ K84

♠ 7
♡ KQJ10632
◇ 1094
♣ 95

♠ KJ83
♡ 987
◇ 72
♣ AQJ3

♠ A1095
♡ A5
◇ J63
♣ 10762

West	North	East	South
	1◇	Pass	1♠
3♡	3♠	Pass	4♠

There is no all-purpose formula for defenders with strong trumps. In this hand, a side queen was more relevant than the queen of trumps. West led the king of hearts to the ace. Declarer ruffed a heart in dummy and led the queen of spades to the king and ace. Declarer played the ten of spades.

If East played the jack and returned a diamond or a trump, declarer would finesse the ♠83 in East with ♠95 in hand, draw trumps, and claim, scoring three trumps, one ruff, the ace of hearts, and five diamonds. If East played the jack and returned a heart, declarer would ruff in dummy, pitching a club in hand. He would play a diamond to his jack, cash the nine of spades, and play diamonds. If East resisted ruffing, declarer would have ten tricks. But if East ruffed, he would have only clubs left and would have to give dummy a club trick. Declarer would lose two trumps and a club.

East therefore ducked the ten of spades. Declarer played the ace of diamonds and forwarded the last spade in dummy. If East played the jack, he could play his last heart. After ruffing in hand, declarer played out the diamonds. Again, once East ruffed, he would have only clubs left and would have to give dummy a club trick for the contract, minus 620. East therefore ducked the third spade. Declarer played out his diamonds. East ruffed the third round and led a heart. Declarer had to ruff and was stripped down to only clubs. When he led a small club, West rose with the nine, sealing declarer's fate. If declarer passed the ten of clubs through, East would duck and take the last three tricks with his clubs.

It demanded countless ducks to set the contract. No East managed this feat. The ducks could strip declarer down to clubs, rather than being stripped by declarer. Stripping was an old wine. The difficulty was resisting the itchy feeling to win an earlier trick with your strong trumps and remembering the gadget of a stripping chase, an advanced test in endplay.

Familiar trump faces

2007 NEC Cup
Netherlands v UK/Norway
N/ Neither vulnerable

♠ —	
♡ KJ10743	
◇ Q743	
♣ 542	

♠ AK87		♠ 109653	
♡ Q962		♡ A	
◇ 92		◇ AK85	
♣ J109		♣ K87	

	♠ QJ42
	♡ 85
	◇ J106
	♣ AQ63

West	North	East	South
Helgemo	Jacobs	Armstrong	Schollaardt
	2♡	Double	Pass
3♠	Pass	4♠	
Bertens	Justin Hackett	Bakkeren	Jason Hackett
	3♡	Double	Pass
4♠			

Defending with QJ fourth of trumps can be a nightmare. The popular contract for this hand was 4♠. North led a club to the queen when dummy ducked. South cashed the ace of clubs.

In Australia v Poland, Zmudzinski of Poland returned a club. Declarer played a spade to the ace, noting the 4-0 break. He crossed to the ace of hearts, and advanced a spade. South split his queen. Declarer took the queen with his king, cashed the top diamonds, ruffed a diamond, ruffed a heart, and led the fourth diamond from dummy. South had ♠J4. Declarer (West) had ♠7. Dummy had ♠109. If South ruffed small, declarer would overruff and South would score only the ♠J. If South discarded, declarer would ruff. Each player had two cards left. Dummy scored a spade to make the contract. The play at other tables was similar.

In the first room, North led a small diamond to the ace in dummy. Declarer played the ace of spades and passed the jack of clubs to the queen. South was Schollaardt of Netherlands. He continued with the ten of diamonds to the king in dummy. A spade was led. Schollaardt did not split his trumps, the real divergence from other defenders. Declarer gratefully took the spade with his seven, crossed to the ace of hearts, and played the king of clubs to the ace. South continued a third diamond. Declarer ruffed with his eight. Declarer (West) had ♠K ♡Q96 ♣10. South had ♠QJ ♡5 ♣63. Dummy had ♠1096 ♢8 ♣8. If declarer ruffed the fourth diamond, the ♠QJ scored two tricks for down one. He ruffed a heart, crossed to his ten of clubs, and ruffed another heart. South overruffed and played a trump, exhausting, those of declarer and dummy. Declarer had to lose his remaining heart for minus 50. Declarer would have made his contract if South had three hearts and three clubs.

Schollaardt realised that his ♠QJ scored a trick. As declarer needed to ruff two diamonds in hand, splitting his spade honours seemed futile. He also could overruff dummy in hearts. Once you realise that declarer needs to ruff two diamonds, the "Dutch duck" is dictated. Netherlands won the event.

A scented ruff

		♠ A98	
2000 USA		♡ 8	
Spingold knockout teams		◊ KQ10975	
W/ Both vulnerable		♣ Q54	

	♠ —		♠ J10432
	♡ QJ10542		♡ K63
	◊ 8632		◊ A4
	♣ 972		♣ 1086

		♠ KQ765	
		♡ A97	
		◊ J	
		♣ AKJ3	

West	*North*	*East*	*South*
Soloway	Weichsel	Hamman	Sontag
Pass	1◊	Pass	1♠
Pass	2◊	Pass	2NT (ask)
Pass	3♡ (3-1-6-3)	Pass	4NT
Pass	5◊	Pass	6♠

The question of splitting trumps moves to J10 fifth. Here, a defender held a side ace against a slam. Based on the bidding by North, West led a club rather than a heart. Sontag let the lead run to his ace. He led a spade to the ace, discovering the 5-0 break, and continued with the nine. East covered with the ten, taken by the queen. Declarer led the jack of diamonds to the king in dummy. East played the ace and returned a heart to the ace. Declarer crossed to dummy with the queen of clubs to play diamonds, discarding a heart. East had ♠J43. Declarer (South) had ♠K76. Dummy had ♠8. East ruffed the third round of diamonds. Declarer overruffed, ruffed a heart in dummy, and continued diamonds, overruffing when East ruffed, drew trumps, and claimed 1430. If East had discarded on the third diamond, declarer would have discarded his remaining heart, played the ♠8, and continued diamonds to operate a trump coup against ♠J4 in East.

What if East does not split his trumps? He retains ♠J104, and not ♠J43. He takes the first diamond with his ace and draws a trump with the ten. This removes a potential ruff and entry in dummy. The queen of clubs is the sole entry in dummy to run the diamonds. East has ♠J4 and ruffs the third round of diamonds. Declarer overruffs and has to lose a heart. With ♠J43, East cannot play the jack without losing the hand. If he leads a small spade to the ♠8 in dummy, declarer succeeds along the lines described. Retention of ♠J104 is important when you smell the scent of a heart ruff and assess the shape of declarer. Declarer cannot ruff a heart in dummy before playing diamonds. Defenders have a heart to cash.

A defensive trump squeeze

2007 European Club cup
Poland/ Russia v Hungary
E/ EW vulnerable

	♠ Q53		
	♡ Q9843		
	◇ AQJ		
	♣ Q2		
♠ KJ98		♠ A742	
♡ —		♡ J1062	
◇ 1086		◇ 52	
♣ A109763		♣ J85	
	♠ 106		
	♡ AK75		
	◇ K9743		
	♣ K4		

West	North	East	South
Hommonay	Gromov	Winkler	Dubinin
		Pass	1◇
Pass	1♡	Pass	2♡
Pass	4♡		
Zmudzinski	Macskasy	Balicki	Lakatos
		Pass	1◇
1NT*	Double	2◇ (major)	Double
2♠	3♡	Pass	4♡

*4-card major + a longer minor suit

This hand featured four defence trumps headed by the jack ten. With no bidding to guide him, East in the first room led a diamond. Declarer won and led the queen of hearts. When West showed out, declarer finessed towards his AK7 of hearts. East inserted his jack to the ace. Declarer returned to hand to repeat the finesse in hearts. He drew trumps and discarded two spades on the long diamonds. He lost a spade and a club, making 450.

The defenders in the other room were well known. Their Polish 1NT takeout steered East to lead a club to the ace. West attacked spade with the jack to the queen and ace. East continued a spade to the king. The third spade forced a ruff in dummy. The safety play in the trumps vaporised. Unless declarer led a heart to the seven on the first trump, he went down. This enterprising defensive trump squeeze is termed a "punch." Defenders executed four thunderous punches to save their delicate trumps.

A submarine in heaven

1991 USA	♠ J1098		
Rubber bridge	♡ QJ10		
E/ NS vulnerable	◊ K98		
	♣ AK3		

♠ 765	♠ AKQ432
♡ —	♡ 543
◊ 76432	◊ AJ10
♣ QJ854	♣ 2

♠ —
♡ AK98762
◊ Q5
♣ 10976

West	North	East	South
	P Pavlicek		R Pavlicek
		1♠	2♡
2♠	4♡	4♠	5♡
Pass	6♡		

Squeezing declarer in trumps is a wonder in bridge; squeezing declarer on the first trick is a miracle. Any East would cover the jack in dummy when partner led a spade. Declarer ruffed, crossed to the ten of hearts, and led a small diamond, Morton's fork. East ducked. Winning the trick with the queen, declarer crossed to the jack of hearts and played a spade. East covered and declarer ruffed. Based on the bidding and play, declarer decided that East was short in clubs and West had the queen and jack of clubs, a Queen Discovery.

Declarer drew trumps and advanced the ten of clubs, covered by the queen and king. Declarer led a third spade from dummy, covered by East, and ruffed in hand. The fourth spade in dummy was now good. Declarer led the nine of clubs, covered by the jack and ace. The fourth spade discarded a diamond. The ♣76 in hand lost a trick to the ♣85 in West. Pavlicek played faultlessly, fulfilling the slam.

Suppose that if, after the first trump to dummy and a diamond continuation, East rises with his ace. Declarer takes the return and crosses to dummy twice. He leads spades twice to ruff out the top spades in East. He cashes the queen of diamonds and crosses to dummy with a top club. The king of diamonds and the fourth spade provide discards for two losing clubs. In actual play, East ducked when the second spade was led. Declarer discarded his remaining diamond and ruffed a diamond in hand, and proceeded with the club play as described.

Ducking a spade by East was actually the only defence, but *on the first trick*. It squeezes declarer for a suitable discard. If declarer discards a diamond, East rises with the ace on the first diamond, smothering the queen. The king can park a club. There remains a club loser. The ♠1098 in dummy, facing an earthly ♠AKQ in East, cannot provide a further spade trick. If declarer discards a club on the first trick, East ducks when a diamond is led from dummy. The diamond and club loser cannot escape. This defence of forcing declarer into a premature discard, termed a "submarine," is not new. East knew from the bidding that South had a void in spades. The diamond positions were the familiar Morton's fork. The recommended defence to a fork is a submarine.

A holy angel in heaven, flying high in a submarine, might find the divine duck on the first spade. "We all live in a yellow submarine" is a lyric from a Beatles song. Yes, we can—and find a similar duck in our next adventure.